#1 *NEW YORK TIMES* BESTSELLING AUTHOR

# MIKE EVANS

# THE

# SEVEN FEASTS

# OF ISRAEL

TimeWorthy
BOOKS

P.O. Box 30000, Phoenix, AZ 85046

*The Seven Feasts of Israel*

Copyright © 2016 All rights reserved Printed in the United States of America

Published by TimeWorthy Books
P. O. Box 30000
Phoenix, AZ 85046

Design: Peter Gloege | LOOK Design Studio

Hardcover:   978-1-62961-113-6
Paperback:   978-1-62961-114-3
   Canada:   978-1-62961-115-0

The book is dedicated to my good friend,
**Dr. Mark Rutland.**

Mark is founder of the National Institute on Christian
Leadership, which is attended by my son, Michael
(CEO of Friends of Zion Museum in Jerusalem).
Mark has served as president of two universities,
as pastor and associate pastor of three of America's
megachurches, and is founder of Global Servants,
a worldwide missionary organization.

# PART ONE

# PART TWO

# PART I

## GOD'S PATTERN
## FOR HIS PEOPLE

# INTRODUCTION

T he seven major feasts set forth by Jehovah in the Old
Testament book of Leviticus give a cadence, a pattern
to the lives of the Jewish people. These holy days reassure
the celebrants of God's divine order, piety, and supreme
worthiness. Jehovah cares for and watches over His people.
The feasts have provided a thread of continuity for the Israelites from the moment of their escape from Egypt, as well
as offering comfort, hope, and encouragement in times of
trouble. The purpose of the seven observances is to turn the
focus of the people to salvation and redemption through the
Messiah. The significance of the feasts, however, reaches
beyond the borders of the nation of Israel and circles the
globe—wherever mankind needs a prophetic and redemp-
tive message.

# CHAPTER 1

*And Abraham said, My son, God will provide
himself a lamb for a burnt offering: so
they went both of them together.*

GENESIS 22:8 KJV

The Old Testament book of Leviticus, chapter 23, introduces the seven feasts the children of Israel were to observe annually. In verse two, the word *feast* can be translated as the Hebrew word *mo'ed.*[1] This may be a bit confusing, as many tend to picture a festival as a large gathering complete with quantities of food and a carnival-like atmosphere. In actuality, the word has a much deeper meaning: appointed time or season, appointed place, appointed meeting. We first see mo'ed in Genesis 1:14 in reference to the establishment of seasons during the Creation. In Leviticus, it might be suggested that the phrase "ceremonial assembly" better describes the essence of the word. The gatherings ordered by Jehovah may sometimes have called for a celebratory meal, but that was not the primary objective of the convocation. The function of these feasts was and is to provide a representation of God's plan—in a chosen time, a chosen place, and for a very precise purpose.

In verse six, another Hebrew word is used: *chag*, a derivative of the word *chagag*.[2] It means to "move in a circle; to march in a sacred procession, celebrate, dance, to keep a solemn feast." God did not ordain the observing of the various festivals to give the Israelites seven occasions to party; rather, they were to be a framework for His plan of redemption for mankind. They were designed to show His chosen people a foreshadowing of the coming of the Messiah and His role in that plan.

## THE FEASTS INTRODUCED

Since God is a God of order, the feasts did not occur haphazardly, but annually and according to the Hebrew calendar: Passover, Unleavened Bread, Firstfruits, Feast of Weeks or Pentecost, Feast of Trumpets, Day of Atonement, and the Feast of Tabernacles. In Leviticus 23, the feasts appear in the following verses:

Passover—verse 5

Unleavened Bread—verse 6

Firstfruits—verse 10

Pentecost—verses 15–16

Feast of Trumpets—verse 24

Day of Atonement—verse 27

Feast of Tabernacles—verse 34

God's flawless order of events reveals His holiness and His demands that we worship Him in certain ways. First Chronicles 16:29 (NIV) reveals how we are to respond to Jehovah:

Ascribe to the LORD the glory due his name; bring an offering and come before him. Worship the LORD in the splendor of his holiness.

Mankind cannot worship a holy God any other way— except through righteousness and holiness. Why? He requires that we worship according to His precepts. He is, after all, a God who demands order, and He reveals that to His people beginning in Genesis through the last chapter of Deuteronomy. A holy God commands respect and veneration, reverence in worship, and devout consecration. But what does it mean to worship God in the beauty of His holiness?

How can we mere mortals hope to be holy enough to worship Jehovah?

Dr. Jack Hayford, chancellor of The King's University in Van Nuys, California, provides an answer. He said:

> I wondered how you got beautiful enough to worship God. The Bible, in speaking of the beauty of holiness, is speaking of a **beauty that flows out of worship**. The idea of worship is intended to **cultivate** something in us . . . . Now *this* is the beauty of worship.
>
> That **in the presence** of a God of all holiness, we might come, even though there is so much insufficiency in us and things that make us feel unworthy. **As we worship**, He will come and touch us with His life and power, and as He does, **He qualifies us** for our tomorrows . . . . In the beauty of the holiness of worship, we come and see His awesome holiness, which is **His wholeness disposed in favor of our brokenness and inadequacy.** (Emphasis in the original.)[3]

## AN OUTLINE FOR WORSHIP

The institution of the seven major feasts was intended to cultivate within God's creation the desire to worship Him. The holy convocations were not only public; they were a memorial to Jehovah's deliverance and provision. The nation was called together in a sacred assembly to observe, to celebrate, and to praise their Creator. At each meeting, the people were reminded of what He had done for them in delivering them from the hand of Pharaoh in Egypt and leading them to the land promised to Abraham and his offspring. Stories of Jehovah's deliverance in the desert, opening a pathway through the sea, fighting their battles, giving the Ten Commandments to Moses, toppling the walls of Jericho, and others were told and retold. (It must be remembered that, in early times, all knowledge was passed down from generation to generation only through the spoken word.) These festivals and feasts helped to reveal, underscore, and amplify this knowledge of how God desires mankind to worship Him. Within these accounts were valuable lessons on sin, judgment, faith, and forgiveness.

Seven is God's number of fullness, perfection, and completion. In Genesis 2:2–3 (NKJV), the importance of the number seven is stressed:

And on the seventh day God ended His work which He had done, and He rested on the seventh day from all His work which He had done. Then God blessed the seventh day and sanctified it, because in it He rested from all His work which God had created and made.

Perhaps the most detailed showcase is found in the book of Revelation—sometimes referred to as the "Book of Sevens"—where God revealed to John seven churches, letters, spirits, lampstands, stars, seals, horns, angels, trumpets, thunders, crowns, plagues, golden bowls, and kings. In the seven feasts, we see the portrayal of death, deliverance, salvation, provision, praise, empowerment, and safety. Most of the feasts have fulfilled prophecies regarding the coming of the Messiah; a few have not.

Over time and with the Diaspora, the festivals eventually became only a series of empty ceremonies and were subject to condemnation by the prophets, those men in Israel who were called upon to deliver God's Word to the people. The prophet Isaiah delivered a scathing indictment to the Israelites in Isaiah 1:11–14 (NKJV):

"To what purpose is the multitude of your sacrifices to Me?" Says the Lord. "I have had enough of burnt offerings of rams and the fat of fed cattle. I do not delight in the blood of bulls, or of lambs or goats. When you come to appear before Me, who has required this from your hand, to trample My courts? Bring no more futile sacrifices; incense is an abomination to Me. The New Moons, the Sabbaths, and the calling of assemblies—I cannot endure iniquity and the sacred meeting. Your New Moons and your appointed feasts My soul hates; they are a trouble to Me, I am weary of bearing them."

In 1 Samuel 15, God gave specific instructions to King Saul to destroy the Amalekites—sparing no one and no animal. Saul almost fulfilled Jehovah's instructions; but being *almost* obedient is not being completely compliant. Rather than destroying everything in his path, Saul spared the Amalekite king and the best of the animals. When Samuel the prophet approached the Israelite encampment, he heard the lowing of cattle and the bleating of sheep. Marching into Saul's presence, Samuel demanded to know why the

Israelite king had not followed God's direction. Like many a leader, Saul first blamed it on his troops and then tried to buy God's favor:

> But they are going to sacrifice them to the Lord your God. We have destroyed everything else. 1 Samuel 15:15 NLT

Far from being pleased with Saul's response, Samuel had some harsh news for the ruler:

> What is more pleasing to the Lord: your burnt offerings and sacrifices or your obedience to his voice? Listen! Obedience is better than sacrifice, and submission is better than offering the fat of rams. Rebellion is as sinful as witchcraft, and stubbornness as bad as worshiping idols. So because you have rejected the command of the Lord, he has rejected you as king . . . . Since you have rejected the Lord's command, he has rejected you as king of Israel. 1 Samuel 15:22–23, 26b NLT

Rebellion not only robbed Saul of his kingdom, it ultimately deprived the Israelites of their relationship with

Jehovah. Not all turned aside from worshiping God; not all were deprived of hearing His voice. Some remained faithful; some followed His precepts. Many, however, were left to wander aimlessly away from the One who loved them despite their sins. He would prove that love in the most unexpected of ways, and even then only a remnant would believe.

## THE SCARLET THREAD

The encounter between Rahab and the Israelite spies in Joshua 2:9 and their response in Joshua 2:18 (KJV) provides another illustration of the salvation offered by Jehovah:

> And she said unto the men, I know that
> the Lord hath given you the land, and that
> your terror is fallen upon us, and that all
> the inhabitants of the land faint because of
> you . . . . Behold, when we come into the land,
> thou shalt bind this line of scarlet thread in
> the window which thou didst let us down
> by: and thou shalt bring thy father, and thy
> mother, and thy brethren, and all thy father's
> household, home unto thee.

The scarlet cord suspended from Rahab's window was symbolic of her faith in the God of the Israelites, representative of her belief in the stories she had heard of His power and deliverance. She had not only chanced the loss of her life, but those of her family by hiding the Hebrew spies and providing a way of escape for them. Her reward was a place in the lineage of Christ as the mother of Boaz, the great-great-grandfather of David.

There is a scarlet thread interwoven through the pages of the Old Testament. It, and the prophecies also contained therein, present an unimpeachable picture of the Messiah from birth to death and resurrection. His birth in Bethlehem was foretold in Micah 5:2 (KJV):

> But thou, Bethlehem Ephratah, though thou be little among the thousands of Judah, yet out of thee shall he come forth unto me that is to be ruler in Israel; whose goings forth have been from of old, from everlasting.

Messiah was to be born of a virgin:

> Therefore the Lord himself shall give you a sign; Behold, a virgin shall conceive, and

bear a son, and shall call his name Immanuel.

Isaiah 7:14 KJV

In other scriptures, we read that there would be a forerunner (Malachi 4:5–6; Isaiah 40:3); the Messiah would be rejected by men and crucified with criminals (Isaiah 53). Psalm 22 presents a detailed picture of the crucifixion. These are only a few of the more than three hundred prophecies given hundreds and sometimes thousands of years before the coming of the Messiah. Jesus fulfilled each one during his thirty-three years on Earth. He would be welcomed by some, rejected by others: "But as many as received him, to them gave he power to become the sons of God, even to them that believe on his name." John 1:12 KJV.

Jesus completed the Feast of the Passover when He was crucified. When He was placed in a tomb borrowed from Joseph of Arimathaea, the Feast of Unleavened Bread was realized. The Feast of Firstfruits was satisfied when Jesus rose from the dead; and the Feast of Pentecost was accomplished following Christ's ascension in Acts chapter 2 as the approximately 120 gathered in the upper room were filled with the Holy Spirit. Only three feasts remain to be fulfilled in the present day: Feast of Trumpets, Day of Atonement, and Feast of Tabernacles.

God's plan did not begin with the birth of a baby in Bethlehem; it began before He laid out the foundation of the world and spoke it into being. Jehovah provided a perfect picture of the plan when He gave Moses the design for the feast days to be observed by the Israelites. He wanted them to see the shadow of what was to come, and revealed it to prophets, priests, and kings long before the angel appeared to a young virgin named Mary. The prophet Amos inscribed:

> Surely the Lord God does nothing, unless
> He reveals His secret to His servants the
> prophets. Amos 3:7 NKJV

God's timing is never random, something left to the whim of mankind. No, it is the meticulous unfolding of a covenant plan that began in Genesis and will conclude with the last verse of Revelation. In all sixty-six books, we are presented with one snapshot after another of the revelation of Jehovah's grace and mercy and His plan of redemption through Jesus, the Messiah.

In succeeding chapters, we will examine each feast, how it was established, the meaning associated with a particular festival, and how it points to those prophecies concerning the Messiah.

# CHAPTER 2

*These are the feasts of the Lord, holy convocations*
*which you shall proclaim at their appointed*
*times. On the fourteenth day of the first*
*month at twilight is the Lord's Passover.*

LEVITICUS 23:4–5 NKJV

Exodus, the second book of the Pentateuch, is the story of deliverance from bondage and of restoration—the establishing of a special relationship between Jehovah and the children of Israel and the first Passover. It is the story of Moses and his birth, life, and sudden departure from Egypt after murdering an Egyptian overseer (see Exodus 2:11–12). Moses fled to the desert of Midian where God hardened him to desert life in the place he would spend the second forty years of his existence. The adopted son of Pharaoh's daughter learned meekness and humility and, at the same time, grew physically stronger for the task that, unbeknownst to him, lay ahead. At the end of forty years on the backside of the desert, Moses was charged by Yahweh with stalking into the throne room of Pharaoh, the most powerful man in the vast region, and demanding that his Israelite bond slaves be allowed to pack up and leave Goshen, the area to which they had been assigned.

As he returned to Egypt Moses encountered Aaron, his blood brother, in the desert. The two men made their way to the palace to challenge Pharaoh. With the ruler's refusal to let the Israelites go, God began to visit ten plagues on the land. Rather than persuade the ruler, it achieved the opposite effect and the burdens that had been placed on the children of Jacob were intensified. The last plague, the death of all of Egypt's firstborn, was the final straw for the rebellious Pharaoh.

Beginning in Exodus 11:4 (NKJV), it is written that Moses and Aaron were sent to warn the Egyptian ruler of the last terrible plague that was to be poured out upon the land and its people:

> "Thus says the Lord: 'About midnight I
> will go out into the midst of Egypt; and all
> the firstborn in the land of Egypt shall die,
> from the firstborn of Pharaoh who sits on his

throne, even to the firstborn of the female servant who is behind the handmill, and all the firstborn of the animals. Then there shall be a great cry throughout all the land of Egypt, such as was not like it before, nor shall be like it again. But against none of the children of Israel shall a dog move its tongue, against man or beast, that you may know that the Lord does make a difference between the Egyptians and Israel.' And all these your servants shall come down to me and bow down to me, saying, 'Get out, and all the people who follow you!' After that I will go out." Then he went out from Pharaoh in great anger.

Moses was vitally aware of what was about to befall the Egyptian people. Remember, as a baby he was saved by Pharaoh's daughter because of an edict that demanded the deaths of all babies born to the children of Israel. Because of that action and the king's refusal to free God's people, a dire penalty would be exacted not only on Pharaoh's household but also on each family in the land of Egypt. Harsh, yes, but Pharaoh had been given numerous opportunities to heed the voice of Jehovah. Because God is a God of love, He made a way for the Israelites to escape the sentence of death that had been pronounced.

In Exodus 12, Moses delivered the instructions from Jehovah on the selection of the perfect lamb in preparation for the tenth and final plague. The animal, without spot or blemish, was to be chosen and removed from the flock on the tenth day of the month. It was to be watched carefully for four days to ensure that Jehovah's directions were followed completely. The owner was to feed and lovingly care for the lamb. The relationship between the owner and the lamb was to be one of affection. Why? God wanted His people to realize that an innocent lamb would be sacrificed so that the household could be saved. Imagine how carefully the lamb must have been chosen and with what regret it was slain!

The night before the Passover lamb was to be offered and its blood applied to the doorposts of the homes of every Israelite, Jehovah sent them forth to their neighbors, giving them specific instructions and great favor:

> And the Lord said to Moses, "I will bring
> one more plague on Pharaoh and on Egypt.
> Afterward he will let you go from here. When
> he lets you go, he will surely drive you out of

here altogether. Speak now in the hearing of the people, and let every man ask from his neighbor and every woman from her neighbor, articles of silver and articles of gold." And the Lord gave the people favor in the sight of the Egyptians. Moreover the man Moses was very great in the land of Egypt, in the sight of Pharaoh's servants and in the sight of the people. Exodus 11:1–3 NKJV

What incredible favor extended to this group of slaves! What would your reaction be if someone knocked on your door and politely asked for your gold and silver—assuming you had any available? God had paved the way for His people to survive financially—even in the face of Pharaoh's antagonism and acrimony. When the knock sounded on the door, the Egyptian captors readily gave to the Israelites. In Exodus 3:21–22 (NKJV), we see another description of this event:

And I will give this people favor in the sight of the Egyptians; and it shall be, when you go, that you shall not go empty-handed. But every woman shall ask of her neighbor, namely, of her who dwells near her house, articles of silver, articles of gold, and clothing;

and you shall put them on your sons and on your daughters. So you shall plunder the Egyptians.

## FROM DEPRIVATION TO PROVISION

Years of deprivation and disfavor culminated in one night of provision and preferential treatment. Joseph's ancestors were set free bearing the blessings of Jehovah as they hurriedly followed Moses to the Red Sea. Psalm 105:37 recounts, "He also brought them out with *silver and gold*, and there was *none feeble* among His tribes" (emphasis mine, NKJV). In the midst of their captivity, Jehovah-Mephalti—the Lord my Deliverer—blessed His people with both health and wealth.

Moses discovered that the favor of Jehovah God opens doors that no man can shut! It provided material goods that would never have been offered to the suffering Israelites while in bondage to the Egyptians. Can you picture those who opened their doors to the knocks of their Hebrew neighbors? How they might have bowed and then hurried back inside to fulfill the requests of their hated, and now feared, enemies?

Was this abundance of wealth provided simply to line the pockets of the Israelites—to pay them back for all the years of hard labor under the harsh reign of Pharaoh? No, it was for a greater purpose: God would eventually ask that His people open their hearts and coffers to provide the materials needed to build and furnish the tabernacle.

God had given Moses very specific instructions regarding the tenth and final plague that was to grip the land of Egypt. In Exodus 12:1–14 (NIV), Jehovah set forth the precise instructions that were to be followed by the Hebrew children:

> The Lord said to Moses and Aaron in Egypt, "This month is to be for you the first month, the first month of your year. Tell the whole community of Israel that on the tenth day of this month each man is to take a lamb for his family, one for each household. If any household is too small for a whole lamb, they must share one with their nearest neighbor, having taken into account the number of people there are. You are to determine the amount of lamb needed in accordance with what each person will eat. The animals you choose must be year-old males without defect, and you may take them from the sheep or the goats. Take care of them until the fourteenth

day of the month, when all the members of the community of Israel must slaughter them at twilight. Then they are to take some of the blood and put it on the sides and tops of the doorframes of the houses where they eat the lambs. That same night they are to eat the meat roasted over the fire, along with bitter herbs, and bread made without yeast. Do not eat the meat raw or boiled in water, but roast it over a fire—with the head, legs and internal organs. Do not leave any of it till morning; if some is left till morning, you must burn it. This is how you are to eat it: with your cloak tucked into your belt, your sandals on your feet and your staff in your hand. Eat it in haste; it is the Lord's Passover. On that same night I will pass through Egypt and strike down every firstborn of both people and animals, and I will bring judgment on all the gods of Egypt. I am the Lord. The blood will be a sign for you on the houses where you are, and when I see the blood, I will pass over you. No destructive plague will touch you when I strike Egypt. This is a day you are to commemorate; for the generations to come you shall celebrate it as a festival to the Lord—a lasting ordinance."

## SALVATION THROUGH THE PASSOVER LAMB

With a lamb, God had provided a way of escape for His people—an exchange for the firstborn in each family. Obedience was all that was required for the death angel to pass over Israelite homes. Jehovah then instructed that as a reminder of His graciousness, the Israelites were to observe a memorial day annually and in perpetuity—Passover. God stated in precise detail how the event was to be observed:

- ✧ The lamb was to be selected and carefully tended until the appointed time.

- ✧ It was to be slaughtered and its blood collected in a basin. It was to be roasted and totally consumed—anything left over was to be burned with fire.

- ✧ Its blood was to be brushed on the lintel and doorposts of the home with a branch of hyssop. Can you picture the care that must have been taken by the head of the

household to be sure the lintel and doorposts were painstakingly covered with
the blood of the lamb? Christian writer—
and carpenter by trade—George Warnock wrote of the significance of hyssop
in the Passover observance:

Why the hyssop? Because it was so insignificant and
ordinary . . . and easily within the reach of all. God would
have us to know that no man is excluded from His grace
because of what he lacks in himself. Nor is he excused
because of what he lacks by nature; or because of environ-
ment, upbringing, background, social stature, weakness,
poverty, or ignorance. We might accuse ourselves because
of these things, or excuse ourselves for our lack of them.
But God would have us to know that . . . if there be in the
standards of men such distinctions that would make some
to be superior to others, then if he would know the covering
of the Blood he must apply the Blood by the same token
as his lowly brother. He must use the "hyssop." It is just a
lowly shrub. It is a bitter herb, and is known to have certain
medicinal properties. It has purplish flowers—beautiful in its
own right . . . low growing, and fragrant . . . if one would stoop
low enough to appreciate it. But the use of the hyssop was
not optional. There could be no distinction here; nor could

there be any standard that would cause certain exclusions. It had to be hyssop because we must know that in the sight of God there is no act of the will, no refinement of character, no manner of good works or appearances before God that would ensure the covering of the Blood on our behalf. The hyssop would speak of that humiliation and abasement of the human will before God—a bitter medicine as far as the sickly human heart is concerned—but fragrant and beautiful in the sight of God as He stoops low to heal the broken and the contrite heart.[4]

✧ The unleavened bread is symbolic of the haste of the Israelites' departure from Egypt—the lack of sufficient time for the dough to rise.

✧ The bitter herbs represent the harsh treatment received at the hands of their cruel Egyptian taskmasters. Might this also be symbolic of the bitter tears shed by the children of Israel during their captivity? Or the cries of the mothers as their children were born and then immediately murdered by the midwives? It might have been indicative of the groanings as backs were lashed by whips or bent beneath the heavy load laid upon the Israelites. Such deep and abiding bitterness was the result of four hundred years of pain and agony for the children of Israel.

✧ The people were to be fully clothed while eating the meal. They needed to be ready for the trek before them— cloaks donned, sandals fastened, and staff in hand.

God had already promised in Exodus 6:6–7 (ESV):

> Say therefore to the people of Israel, 'I am the Lord, and I will bring you out from under the burdens of the Egyptians, and I will deliver you from slavery to them, and I will redeem you with an outstretched arm and with great acts of judgment. I will take you to be my people, and I will be your God, and you shall know that I am the Lord your God, who has brought you out from under the burdens of the Egyptians.

## THE SEDER CEREMONY

Today, as the Jewish people prepare for the feast, every vestige of yeast is removed from the home. In the days before the Passover observance, Jewish dwellings must be cleansed of anything containing *chametz* or leaven. Not only is it symbolic of the speed with which the Israelites were chased out of Egypt, it is a "symbolic way of removing the 'puffiness' (arrogance, pride) from our souls."[5] This picture of puffiness might also be labeled "self-righteousness."

*The Message* has an excellent interpretation of 1 Corinthians 5:6–8:

> Your flip and callous arrogance in these things bothers me. You pass it off as a small thing, but it's anything but that. Yeast, too, is a "small thing," but it works its way through a whole batch of bread dough pretty fast. So get rid of this "yeast." Our true identity is flat and plain, not puffed up with the wrong kind of ingredient. The Messiah, our Passover Lamb, has already been sacrificed for the Passover meal, and we are the Unraised Bread part of the feast. So let's live out our part in the feast, not as raised bread swollen with the yeast

of evil, but as flat bread—simple, genuine, unpretentious.

When leaven is added to flour, a chemical reaction causes the bread to increase in volume. Could it be that Jehovah was presenting yet another picture with the unleavened bread? God wanted His people to understand that He alone was the Redeemer, and there was no cause for them to be "puffed up." He was the miracle maker, the rescuer of His people from the bondage of Pharaoh. There was no place in His plan for haughtiness or vanity, just a total reliance on Jehovah-Mephalti—the Lord my Deliverer.

The grains that must be swept from the home are wheat, rye, barley, oats, and spelt—a type of hulled wheat. Some Orthodox Jews also include rice, corn, peanuts, and legumes.[6] These items are not be eaten or even possessed by the homeowner during Passover.

The housecleaning undertaken during the pre-Pesach days is a massive assignment. Every crumb, every speck, and every iota of anything that contains leaven is to be scrubbed away. A few pieces of bread are left behind for the children to discover. These are burned outside the home to rid it of the symbol of sin that pervades daily life. Now the home is ready for the observance.

The Passover Seder, or ceremonial dinner to celebrate the exodus from Egypt, is to be practiced by Jews as an observance—a reminder—of Jehovah's mercy, grace, and deliverance centuries before in Egypt. Individuals seated at the table are to see themselves as being the recipient of God's deliverance and His promises recorded in Exodus 6:6–8:

> "Therefore say to the children of Israel: 'I am the Lord; I will bring you out from under the burdens of the Egyptians, I will rescue you from their bondage, and I will redeem you with an outstretched arm and with great judgments. [The first three promises speak of redemption. The next three promises speak of relationship.] I will take you as My people, and I will be your God. Then you shall know that I am the Lord your God who brings you out from under the burdens of the Egyptians. [The last two promises speak of provision.] And I will bring you into the land which I swore to give to Abraham, Isaac, and Jacob; and I will give it to you as a heritage: I am the Lord.'" Emphasis added, NKJV

As family members gather around the table to celebrate the Seder, the woman of the home lights candles to mark the beginning of the hallowed event. A Seder plate has been readied for the ceremony. It contains the following:

✧ *Karpas from the Greek means "fresh, raw vegetable."* It may be a boiled potato, parsley, or celery.

✧ The roasted shank bone of a lamb, a reminder of the Paschal lamb. *Paschal* means "He [God] skipped over" the houses of the children of Israel.

✧ *Beitzah,* or a hard-boiled egg. The egg is symbolic of mourning and is a reminder of the loss of Solomon's and Herod's temples in Jewish history.

✧ *Charoset,* a paste made of apples, nuts, wine, and spices. It comes from the Hebrew word *cheres,* or clay. It is representative of the mortar for buildings that the Egyptian overseers compelled the Hebrews to craft.

✧ *Maror,* or bitter herbs. This is a reminder of the brutal slavery the Israelites endured under Pharaoh.

✧ In some homes, a small bowl of salt water is placed on the plate as a reminder of the tears shed by the Jews, and of the Red Sea through which God led the Israelites.

After the last candle has been lighted, the person seated at the head of the table raises the first of four cups of wine—this one representing sanctification—and blesses it before partaking. The guests seated at the table recline, or lean to the left, to signify freedom. (In ancient times, only those people who enjoyed freedom reclined as they partook of a meal.)

The leader of the Seder ceremonially washes his hands and then passes a vessel containing salted water around the table. The salt is indicative of the cries of the children of Israel while in captivity. Each person then dips a piece of parsley or lettuce, signifying a new beginning, into the water. Three matzahs are placed into a special bag designed with three separate compartments. (In the matzah prepared today, even centuries after the death of and resurrection of Christ, this symbolism—the piercings and stripes—remain as the picture of Jehovah's perfect plan of salvation.) One matzah is broken with half wrapped in linen and hidden away. A whole matzah is placed in the first and second compartments, and in the third, the *Afikomen*, or part of the broken matzah. It is eaten at the conclusion of the meal as dessert.

The second cup of wine—representative of the plagues—is raised and blessed but not drunk at that moment. A child is selected to ask the age-old question with answers in four parts:

"Why is this night different from all other nights?"

1. On all other nights we may eat chametz and matzah, but on this night—only matzah.

2. On all other nights we eat any vegetables, but on this night—we eat maror [bitter herbs].

3. On all other nights we do not dip even once, but on this night—twice.

4. On all other nights we eat either sitting or reclining, but on this night—we all recline.[7]

## THE BEGINNING OF THE SEDER MEAL

The meal begins with a hard-boiled egg. The story is told of a rabbi who was asked about the inclusion of an egg:

> "Because eggs symbolize the Jew," the
> rabbi answered. "The more an egg is burned
> or boiled, the harder it gets."[8]

At the end of the meal, the Afikomen is removed from the pouch and consumed. It is symbolic of the Pascal Lamb. No other food is eaten for the remainder of the night. The third cup of wine—the cup of redemption—is then drunk. Those at the table sing the second part of the Hallel (a song of praise)—Psalms 115–118—after which the fourth cup of wine, the cup of praise, is consumed. It signifies the end of the Seder, after which point some families add, *"Le-shanah ha-ba'ah bi-Yerushalayim,"* or "Next year in Jerusalem."

This phrase is also infused with hope for the coming of the Messiah. Author Sam Nadler wrote:

> This cup calls us to praise God as we
> remember all that He has done for us. In
> remembering, let us also proclaim and
> rejoice in the true meaning of Passover. The
> head of the house sits opposite an empty

seat traditionally left for Elijah the Prophet. Traditionally, Elijah is expected to arrive at Passover preceding and proclaiming the Coming One, that is, the Messiah Himself . . . This tradition is taken from the book of Malachi. In Malachi 3:1, we read, "Behold, I send My messenger, and he will prepare the way before Me. And the Lord, whom you seek, will suddenly come to His temple, even the Messenger of the covenant, in whom you delight. Behold, He is coming."[9] (NKJV)

Hebrew student Gilad Barach also offered this insight into this cry of hope:

Although Jews pray each day for their immediate redemption, "Next year in Jerusalem" signifies something more—their longing for the return of the holiday sacrifices. Yom Kippur and Passover are unique in the Jewish calendar because, more than any other holiday, their fundamental identities are inherently and integrally bound to the Temple service . . . . Though not despondent as we conclude this festive night, we admit

that the highlight of the seder night is miss-
ing in the Temple's absence . . . . Next year,
we will observe the day properly, in a rebuilt
Jerusalem, with a rebuilt Temple and a reen-
acted sacrificial service.[10]

Perhaps if we could simply catch a glimpse of the city
John saw, Christians might welcome the arrival of a new year
with the words, "This year, New Jerusalem." John, while
exiled on the Isle of Patmos, wrote of the magnificence of
the Jerusalem in his vision:

> Then I, John, saw the holy city, New Jeru-
> salem, coming down out of heaven from God,
> prepared as a bride adorned for her husband.
> And I heard a loud voice from heaven saying,
> "Behold, the tabernacle of God is with men,
> and He will dwell with them, and they shall
> be His people. God Himself will be with them
> and be their God. And God will wipe away
> every tear from their eyes; there shall be no
> more death, nor sorrow, nor crying. There
> shall be no more pain, for the former things
> have passed away." Revelation 21:2–4 NKJV

## BEHOLD THE LAMB

It is impossible to separate Judaism and Christianity. Judaism is the seed that falls onto the ground from which a tree grows. From the seed of Abraham and David came the Messiah, the One "sent" from the Father. Jesus was born to Mary, a Jewess from Nazareth. He closely identified with God's chosen people. He studied with them, walked among them, and ministered to His kinsmen, all the while preaching a universal message of His Father's love and grace.

Thirty-three years after His miraculous birth, fifteen hundred years after the celebration of the very first Passover, Jesus had His disciples prepare a place to celebrate the symbolic meal. In Luke 22:15–16 (NKJV) we read:

> Then [Jesus] said to them, "With fervent desire I have desired to eat this Passover with you before I suffer; for I say to you, I will no longer eat of it until it is fulfilled in the kingdom of God."

This meal was the turning point in His earthly ministry, His last before being betrayed into the hands of the Sanhedrin and ultimately the Romans. According to the late Dr. Harold Hoehner, a professor of New Testament studies at Dallas Theological Institute:

It is thought that the Galileans used a different method of reckoning the Passover than the Judeans. The Galileans and Pharisees used the sunrise to sunrise reckoning whereas the Judeans and Sadducees used the sunset to sunset reckoning.[11]

Thus, Jesus and His disciples could very well have celebrated Passover on Thursday evening, which would have made it possible for Him to be the Pascal Lamb slain before the foundation of the world on Friday. Ken Ham, founder of Answers in Genesis and the Creation Museum in Petersburg, Kentucky, wrote:

> Before the universe was created, before time existed, before man was created, God knew that we (in Adam) would sin. He knew we would rebel against our Creator. And in the wisdom and love of God, in eternity, He predetermined a plan so that we could receive a free gift of salvation. In eternity, God planned for the Son of God to step into history to provide the ultimate sacrifice—the sinless Son of God would suffer sin's penalty of death, be raised from the dead, thus

providing a way of salvation. Hebrews 10:10 declares: "By that will we have been sanctified through the offering of the body of Jesus Christ once for all."[12]

Picture the body of Jesus as it hung on the cross. The wounds He bore were in His head, His hands, and His feet—a depiction of the cross. When the Israelites observed the very first Passover, each head of the house applied blood to the lintel over the door and to the doorposts on either side. It is almost certain that in applying the blood some must have dripped down on the floor, forming a cross. Jesus said, "I am the door."

When faced with a visit from the death angel, the only method of deliverance was through the blood of the lamb being applied to the doorposts of the home. John, the disciple, said of Jesus, "Behold! The Lamb of God who takes away the sin of the world!" (John 1:29 NKJV) Religion doesn't take away the sin of the world. Being charitable doesn't remove the stain of sin. Attending church or being baptized doesn't save anyone. The only way of salvation for the sinner is through repentance and acceptance of the blood sacrifice of Jesus, the Lamb of God. He is the Way, the Truth, and the Life.

# CHAPTER 3

*And on the fifteenth day of the same month is the Feast*
*of Unleavened Bread to the Lord; seven days you must*
*eat unleavened bread. On the first day you shall have*
*a holy convocation; you shall do no customary work on*
*it. But you shall offer an offering made by fire to the*
*Lord for seven days. The seventh day shall be a holy*
*convocation; you shall do no customary work on it.'"*

LEVITICUS 23:6–8 NKJV

Preparation for Passover also spills over into the celebration of the Feast of Unleavened Bread. The home is scrubbed and swept free of any semblance of leavening. The day after Passover is observed, the second of the feasts ordained by Jehovah begins: the Feast of Unleavened Bread. It is the first of the pilgrimage feasts, and also a memorial to the hasty departure of the children of Israel from Egypt. The unleavened bread truly is "fast food." It is made with only flour and water, no yeast; because at the outset of the

Exodus, there was simply no time for the dough to rise before the loaves were baked.

Celebrated on the fifteenth day of Nisan, and beginning the evening following Passover, it is a time for purification and spiritual preparation. While Passover lasts for only one day, the Fast of Unleavened Bread is a seven-day observance. The first and last days are celebrated with a holy convocation and offerings. For the entire week, the children of Israel were to eat only unleavened bread that closely resembled what we today sometimes call matzah. The dough was pierced to prevent it from ballooning from the heat and to make it cook faster, and the grate on which it was cooked left a striped pattern on the bread.

Rabbis have subsequently determined that if the bread could be baked within eighteen minutes from preparation to removal from the grill, it was not to be defiled by yeast. The very things that aided in cooking the unleavened bread were, and still are, symbols initiated by Jehovah before the beginning of time. Old Testament scriptures predicted the Messiah would be pierced:

> "And I will pour out on the house of David
> and the inhabitants of Jerusalem a spirit of
> grace and pleas for mercy, so that, when they

look on me, on him whom they have pierced, they shall mourn for him, as one mourns for an only child, and weep bitterly over him, as one weeps over a firstborn." Zechariah 12:10 ESV

For dogs encompass me; a company of evildoers encircles me; they have pierced my hands and feet. Psalm 22:16 ESV

## SEVEN DAYS OF UNLEAVENED BREAD

It has already been pointed out that leaven is a picture of self-righteousness, of relying on *self* rather than on Jehovah. Leaven is a picture of sin, and seven is emblematic of God's number of completion and holiness. Thus God instructed Moses:

Seven days you shall eat unleavened bread. On the first day you shall remove leaven from your houses. For whoever eats leavened bread from the first day until the seventh day, that person shall be cut off from Israel. On the first day there shall be a holy convocation, and on the seventh day there shall be a holy convocation for you. No manner of work shall be done on them; but that which everyone must eat—that only may be prepared by you. So you shall observe the Feast of Unleavened Bread, for on this same day I will have brought your armies out of the land of Egypt. Therefore you shall observe this day throughout your generations as an everlasting ordinance. Exodus 12:15–17 NKJV

God's chosen ones were to remove leaven from their homes and from their lives for a period of seven days. It was an act of consecration for the year ahead. Yahweh was calling His followers to be righteous, to come out from among the Egyptian world and be a holy people.

The Feast of Unleavened Bread was to forever be a visible reminder that the children of Israel had been totally freed from the world of slavery and sorrow, from the agony of torment by the shedding of the blood of the sacrificial lamb. In chapter 11, verse 4, the prophet Jeremiah referred to Egypt as the "iron furnace." Iron melts at 2,750 degrees, which is incomprehensible to the average person. Yet Jeremiah tells us that the Israelites underwent horrific brutality comparable to that of an iron furnace. Their anguish and affliction was intense.

## A TIME OF REMEMBRANCE

The Feast of Unleavened Bread is for the Israelites a
time of remembrance and a time of hope, a time to put away
sin and self in order to focus on God's graciousness. It is
a prophetic picture of the future, a rehearsal for the time
when the Messiah will come and the unseen will become
visible; true deliverance will become a reality. The prophet
Jeremiah spoke of that coming time:

> "Behold, the days are coming, says the
> Lord, when I will make a new covenant
> with the house of Israel and with the house
> of Judah—not according to the covenant that
> I made with their fathers in the day that I
> took them by the hand to lead them out of
> the land of Egypt, My covenant which they
> broke, though I was a husband to them, says
> the Lord. But this is the covenant that I will
> make with the house of Israel after those
> days, says the Lord: I will put My law in their
> minds, and write it on their hearts; and I will
> be their God, and they shall be My people.
> No more shall every man teach his neighbor,
> and every man his brother, saying, 'Know the

Lord,' for they all shall know Me, from the least of them to the greatest of them, says the Lord. For I will forgive their iniquity, and their sin I will remember no more." Jeremiah 31:31–34 NKJV

On the first and last days of the feast, holy convocations were called. These were days devoted to the worship of Yahweh and the celebration of their deliverance from bondage. No manual labor was to be done except that of food preparation. All the male pilgrims—Hebrew and gentile—who had escaped from Egypt following the Passover were to come together to present a burnt offering, a meal offering, and a sin offering. There were four fixed laws of the Feast of Unleavened Bread:

- ✧ Participation was mandatory.

- ✧ Only unleavened bread could be served.

- ✧ It was an appointed gathering.

- ✧ Each participant was to bring an offering; no one was exempt.

In many instances today, Passover and the Feast of Unleavened Bread are observed by Orthodox Jews as one, rather than two separate occasions. For them it is a time of remembrance, cleansing, and renewal—as well as a time of spiritual preparation. Jehovah never wanted His people to forget from whence they came.

The August 1973 cover of *Ministry* magazine bore a quote by poet and Pulitzer Prize winner Carl Sandburg. He wrote:

> For we know that when a nation goes down
> and never comes back, when a society or a
> civilization perishes, one condition can always
> be found. They forgot from whence they came.
> They lost sight of what brought them along.[13]

## UNLEAVENED BREAD AND JESUS

The Feast of Unleavened Bread that immediately follows Passover is a reminder of the total sinlessness of the Pascal Lamb. A Lamb without blemish is offered on the cross; bread without leavening, the ingredient which is symbolic of sin, is eaten. This is vitally important, for if our Lord had committed just one iniquity, we would have no sacrifice for sin. In 2 Corinthians 5:21 (NKJV), we read:

> For He made Him who knew no sin to be sin
> for us, that we might become the righteous-
> ness of God in Him.

And in John 6:32–35 (NKJV), the disciple reminded us of Jesus' words:

> Then Jesus said to them, "Most assuredly, I say to you, Moses did not give you the bread from heaven, but My Father gives you the true bread from heaven. For the bread of God is He who comes down from heaven and gives life to the world." Then they said to Him, "Lord, give us this bread always." And Jesus said to them, "I am the bread of life. He who comes to Me shall never hunger, and he who believes in Me shall never thirst."

Just as sin must be eradicated from the life of the Believer, so yeast is to be swept from the Jewish home. This tradition is called *Bedikat HaMetz* and is translated as "the search for leaven." Author Edward Chumney wrote of this tradition:

> The preparation for searching and removing the leaven from the house actually begins before Passover (Pesach). First, the wife thoroughly cleans the house to remove all leaven from it. In the Bible, leaven is symbolic of sin.

In cleaning the house, the wife is instructed to purposely leave ten small pieces of leaven (bread) in the house. Then the father takes the children, along with a candle, a wooden spoon, a feather, and a piece of linen cloth, and searches through the house for the ten pieces of leaven. By nightfall on the day before Passover (Pesach), a final and comprehensive search is performed. At this time, the house is completely dark except for the candles. Once the father finds the leaven (bread), he sets the candle down by the leaven and lays the wooden spoon beside the leaven. Then he uses the feather to sweep the leaven onto the spoon. Without touching the leaven, he takes the feather, spoon, and leaven, wraps them in a linen cloth, and casts them out of the door of the house. The next morning (the fourteenth of Nisan), he goes into the synagogue and puts the linen cloth and its contents into a fire to be burned.[14]

The elements used in this traditional search also have meaning: The candle is symbolic of the Word of God (see

Psalm 119:105); the feathers remind us of the Holy Spirit descending as a dove; the spoon is the Lamb in the midst of the throne, which shall feed His people (see Revelation 7:17).

The broken matzah is an emblem of Jesus, who was broken for our sake. Luke 22:19 (ESV) tells us:

> And he took bread, and when he had given thanks, he broke it and gave it to them, saying, "This is my body, which is given for you. Do this in remembrance of me."

Pastor Iain Gordon with Living Waters Church in Tauranga, New Zealand, provided remarkable insight to Jesus' statement:

> Is it not amazing that Jesus would have been taking the second of the three portions of unleavened bread and breaking that? The Jews had performed this year after year but this was the first time that someone had said "This is me! The breaking of this second loaf is me. This is my body which is given and will be broken, for you." Does this not make communion more real? Hopefully it gives you something more to think about when you

next celebrate the Lord's Supper. Actually it is not something that you will think about but someone. The bread of Heaven who came down, was broken, hidden and then found by those who seek Him out! (Emphasis added is mine.)[15]

The Old Testament prophet Micah foretold the place where Jesus was to be born:

> But thou, Bethlehem Ephratah, though thou be little among the thousands of Judah, yet out of thee shall he come forth unto me that is to be ruler in Israel; whose goings forth have been from of old, from everlasting. Micah 5:2 KJV

In Luke 2:4–7 (NKJV), we read:

> Joseph also went up from Galilee, out of the city of Nazareth, into Judea, to the city of David, which is called Bethlehem, because he was of the house and lineage of David, to be registered with Mary, his betrothed wife, who was with child. So it was, that while they were there, the days were completed for her

to be delivered. And she brought forth her firstborn Son, and wrapped Him in swaddling cloths, and laid Him in a manger, because there was no room for them in the inn.

The town of Bethlehem is comprised of two words from the Hebrew: *Beth,* which means "house" and *Lechem,* meaning "bread." And yet another prophecy was fulfilled when the One who is the Bread of Life was born in the House of Bread! Jesus said, "I am the bread of life. He who comes to Me shall never hunger" (John 6:35a NKJV).

# CHAPTER 4

*And the Lord spoke to Moses, saying, "Speak to
the children of Israel, and say to them: 'When
you come into the land which I give to you, and
reap its harvest, then you shall bring a sheaf of
the firstfruits of your harvest to the priest.*

LEVITICUS 23:9–10 NKJV

Passover is a picture drawn by the hand of Jehovah as
a reminder of His redemption. The Feast of Unleavened Bread points His people to a time of purification and
spiritual preparation. It was the offering of a tithe, the first
grains of the harvest, offered to Jehovah with thanksgiving
and gratitude. The Feast of Firstfruits is a table heaped with
the abundance of God's provision.

The events begin with Passover, followed on the second
day by the Feast of Unleavened Bread, and on the third day
is the Feast of Firstfruits. On Passover, a sheaf of barley—the

first crop ready for harvest—was selected and marked as the special sheaf of grain to be presented to the priest in the temple. It was to be harvested the following day, which was the first day of the Feast of Unleavened Bread. It was on the third day that the farmer went into the field to cut and prepare the grain for an offering. The grain was carried to the temple and presented to the priest to be waved before the Lord.

Only twice in Old Testament scripture do we read about the Feast of Firstfruits—in Leviticus 23:9–14 and in Numbers 28:26–31 (NKJV):

Also on the day of the firstfruits, when you bring a new grain offering to the Lord at your Feast of Weeks, you shall have a holy convocation. You shall do no customary work. You shall present a burnt offering as a sweet aroma to the Lord: two young bulls, one ram, and seven lambs in their first year, with their grain offering of fine flour mixed with oil: three-tenths of an ephah for each bull, two-tenths for the one ram, and one-tenth for each of the seven lambs; also one kid of the goats, to make atonement for you. Be sure they are without blemish. You shall present them with their drink offerings, besides the regular burnt offering with its grain offering.

## LAW OF FIRSTFRUITS

Two Old Testament passages outline six foundational decrees to be observed during the Feast of Firstfruits.

In Leviticus 23:10, the Israelites were instructed to observe Firstfruits only after they entered the Promised Land. The sojourn in the wilderness did not allow time for farming or for harvesting that which might have been planted.

Numbers 28:26 and Leviticus 23:11 order the day on which the feast was to be kept. Author and educator John Metzger wrote:

> There was a disagreement between the Pharisees and the Sadducees on this feast. The Pharisees and their rabbinic teachings considered the Passover as a Sabbath, meaning that this feast was to be observed the day after Passover. The Sadducees had the biblical approach which was the first day of the week after the day of Passover. Passover could be

any day of the week, but as the Lord gave the Feast of First Fruits, it was to be only on one day which was the first day of the week after Passover.[16]

The priestly duties were outlined in Leviticus 23:11. The priest was to receive the sheaf of grain and with arms lifted, wave it from side to side as an offering to the Lord.

There were to be three offerings as outlined in Leviticus 23:12–13 and Numbers 28:27–30:

1. Burnt offering—"You shall present a burnt offering as a sweet aroma to the LORD: two young bulls, one ram, and seven lambs in their first year" (v. 27).

2. Meal offering—". . . with their grain offering of fine flour mixed with oil: three-tenths of an ephah for each bull, two-tenths for the one ram, and one-tenth for each of the seven lambs" (vv. 28–29).

3. Drink offering—"You shall present them with their drink offerings" (v. 31).

There was a prohibition associated with the Feast of Firstfruits. The people were forbidden to eat any bread or grain before the wave offering was presented to Jehovah.

In Leviticus 23:14, the command was given that the feast was to be "a statute forever throughout your generations in all your dwellings" (NKJV).

## THE END OF THE OLD FEAST AND A SYMBOLIC NEW BEGINNING

The Feast of Firstfruits ceased to be observed following the Diaspora, the scattering of the Jews to other countries and continents. Jews were then forbidden from owning land and consequently ceased to be farmers. Following the destruction of Herod's temple in AD 70, there was no altar on which to sacrifice burnt offerings, no priests to offer the prescribed gifts to Jehovah, no nation of Israel for nearly 1,900 years. There was no land owned by Jews on which to plant crops, and no harvest from which to choose a sheaf of grain to present to the priests. And so, the Feast of Firstfruits ceased in the form that had been known to the Israelites.

Some of the Israeli *Kibbutzim* (collective communities) have instituted a modern-day celebration of the Feast of Firstfruits. Workers armed with scythes go into the fields of barley and harvest a sheaf of grain. Women follow the harvesters, bundle the grain and place it on flower-bedecked carts. They celebrate with dancing in the fields. When evening falls, the reapers gather in a special procession and make their way to the kibbutz, where the sheaves are stacked in the center of the dining hall. In the absence of a temple and a priest, it is a symbolic offering and an act of praise to Jehovah for His blessing of the harvest.

## THE FEAST FULFILLED

What is the correlation between Firstfruits and Christ? There is no doubt regarding how this celebration mirrors the death and resurrection of our Lord. Among the miracles performed by Jesus were the raising of Jairus' daughter, of Lazarus, and of the widow's son. They were not, however, raised to new life with a glorified body; their earthly bodies were raised. They would, at some time, have to die yet again. Jesus was the firstfruits of a new body, never again to suffer pain, sickness, or death.

The first day of this celebration is three days after Passover. On that day, the sheaf for the wave offering must be presented to the priest. On the third day after Christ arose, he was seen by Mary Magdalene at the tomb. He said to her, "Do not cling to Me, for I have not yet ascended to My Father; but go to My brethren and say to them, 'I am ascending to My Father and your Father, and *to* My God and your God'" (John 20:17 NKJV).

Christ, the ultimate offering—the firstfruits of the resurrection, the supreme harvest, the "perfect sheaf," had to appear before His Father and present himself as a wave offering. Author C. W. Slemming wrote in his book *Thus Shalt Thou Serve: The Feasts and Offerings of Ancient Israel*:

> When the sheaves were cut from the fields and carried to the city, small vacant spots were left behind. When the Lord rose from the dead, He left behind a small vacant spot, which still remains as a reminder of His resurrection—an empty tomb.[17]

The sheaf waved was indicative of the entire harvest; so Jesus' resurrection was a foreshadowing of the final resurrection. He said to the disciples in John 12:24 (NLT), "I tell you the truth, unless a kernel of wheat is planted in the soil and dies, it remains alone. But its death will produce many new kernels—a plentiful harvest of new lives."

You and I are just two of the "many seeds" spoken of by Christ. He died, was buried, and upon His resurrection the way was prepared for all of mankind to respond. When He calls:

...the dead in Christ will rise first. Then we who are alive and remain shall be caught up together with them in the clouds to meet the Lord in the air. And thus we shall always be with the Lord. 1 Thessalonians 4:16b–17 NKJV

Gone forever will be the old body that has been subject to the frailties of this earth! We will have a new body like that of our Savior. The Feast of Unleavened Bread is indicative of having been separated from leaven or sin; the Feast of Firstfruits is symbolic of having been separated or consecrated unto the Lord.

# CHAPTER 5

*And you shall count for yourselves from the day after*
*the Sabbath, from the day that you brought the sheaf of*
*the wave offering: seven Sabbaths shall be completed.*
*Count fifty days to the day after the seventh Sabbath;*
*then you shall offer a new grain offering to the Lord.*

LEVITICUS 23:15–16 NKJV

Fifty days, or seven weeks, following the Feast of Firstfruits, the Feast of Weeks, Shavuot, or Pentecost was
to be celebrated signifying the end of the harvest. Mark
Robinson, editor of *Israel's Messenger* magazine, identified
when the feast was celebrated by the early Jews:

> The Sadducees, generally wealthy members
> of the Jewish aristocracy who had embraced
> Hellenism, were the Temple custodians. They
> numbered about 3,000 at the time of Jesus.
> According to Josephus, in the 107 years from

the beginning of Herod's reign in 37 B.C. to the fall of Jerusalem in 70 A.D., there were 28 high priests. The Talmud records that by the time of Jesus, the high priest bought the office from the government and the position was changed every year. These policies resulted in a group of wealthy Sadducean priestly families being appointed to the office on a regular basis. They understood the Sabbath to refer to the first Saturday of Passover; thus, the counting was to begin on the first Sunday, always putting Pentecost on a Sunday.

The Pharisees generally came from the middle class, were zealous for the Mosaic Law, and were the "party" of the people. At the time of Jesus they numbered about 6,000. They interpreted Sabbath not to mean Saturday but the first day of the rest (the first day of the Passover Festival). The counting would begin on the second day of the Passover Festival and Pentecost could fall on any day. The Pharisees method became the generally accepted method and is used today among the Jewish people.[18]

The feast was to be a holy convocation. Numbers 28:27–31 (ESV) gives us a much more comprehensive list of the types of offerings that were to be made:

> . . . but offer a burnt offering, with a pleasing aroma to the Lord: two bulls from the herd, one ram, seven male lambs a year old; also their grain offering of fine flour mixed with oil, three tenths of an ephah for each bull, two tenths for one ram, a tenth for each of the seven lambs; with one male goat, to make atonement for you. Besides the regular burnt offering and its grain offering, you shall offer them and their drink offering. See that they are without blemish.

In *Rose Guide to the Temple*, author Randall Price explains the meaning of the celebration:

> Fifty days after Passover the Israelites celebrated the Feast of Weeks. This feast is also known as Shavuot, Pentecost, the Feast of Harvest, and the Latter Firstfruits because it was the time to present an offering of new grain of the summer wheat harvest to the

Lord, showing joy and thankfulness for the Lord's blessing of the harvest. It is the second of the three pilgrimages.[19]

According to the Talmud, it does, however, have another, more spiritual meaning. It was on the day of Pentecost that God gave the Torah to the Jews. It also denoted the commencement of a new season of harvest, *Hag HaKatzir* or the "Harvest Holiday." This name was derived from the custom of taking grain to the temple on the feast day.

When Herod's temple was destroyed in AD 70, the celebration of Shavuot became more connected to the giving of the Torah on Mount Sinai. Because of that association, the Ten Commandments are chanted on that day, and some Jews might spend the entire night studying the Torah. Passover released the Israelites from physical bondage to Pharaoh; Shavuot is symbolic of the release from spiritual bondage.

Since about the second century, the practice of reading the book of Ruth during the celebration of Shavuot or Pentecost has been adopted. According to Rev. Mark Robinson of Jewish Awareness Ministries, that custom would play a role in the modern-day church:

For the festival of Shavuot the book of Ruth is read in the synagogue telling the glorious story of the love of a Jewish man for a Gentile woman as he followed the God of Israel's desires. It is no coincidence that at the festival of Shavuot (Pentecost), a Jewish man, Jesus, and ultimately, primarily, a Gentile bride, the church, were brought together, in the birth of the church. This too is a love story of a Jewish man for His Bride![20]

## WHEN THE DAY OF PENTECOST HAD FULLY COME

For New Testament Believers, the day of Pentecost represents the day on which the Holy Spirit was poured out upon those in the Upper Room who were awaiting His arrival and empowerment. Jesus has alerted His disciples of the happening in Acts 1:4–8 (ESV):

And while staying with them he ordered them not to depart from Jerusalem, but to wait for the promise of the Father, which, he said, "you heard from me; for John baptized with water, but you will be baptized with the Holy Spirit not many days from now." So when they had come together, they asked him, "Lord, will you at this time restore the kingdom to Israel?" He said to them, "It is not for you to know times or seasons that the Father has fixed by his own authority. But you will receive power when the Holy Spirit has come upon you, and you will be my witnesses in Jerusalem and in all Judea and Samaria, and to the end of the earth."

The prophet Joel had prophesied that the Spirit would come. Joel chapter one outlines the terrible drought and the plagues that had beset the Israelites and decimated the crops. In chapter two, he advised the people what would happen if they came together to worship and honor Jehovah:

> "And it shall come to pass afterward, that I will pour out my Spirit on all flesh; your sons and your daughters shall prophesy, your old men shall dream dreams, and your young men shall see visions. Even on the male and female servants in those days I will pour out my Spirit." Joel 2:28–29 ESV

As we read in Acts 2:2–4 (ESV), fifty days following Christ's ascension, the disciples were gathered together in a room in Jerusalem:

> And suddenly there came from heaven a sound like a mighty rushing wind, and it filled the entire house where they were sitting. And divided tongues as of fire appeared to them and rested on each one of them. And they were all filled with the Holy Spirit and began to speak in other tongues as the Spirit gave them utterance.

On the day of Pentecost, Peter stood before the assembled multitude and delivered his very first sermon. In Acts 2:40–41 (NKJV), we read of the disciple's call to repentance:

> And with many other words he testified and exhorted them, saying, "Be saved from this perverse generation." Then those who gladly received his word were baptized; and that day about three thousand souls were added to them.

It is interesting to note that 3,000 were saved following Peter's exhortation. Why might that be significant? Let's look back at the giving of the law on Mount Sinai. After Moses received the Ten Commandments written on stone tablets by the very finger of God, he returned to the camp to deliver them to the people waiting at the base of the mountain. But what did he find when he descended out of the cloud? He found a people reveling in rebellion and delighting in disobedience. Having grown weary of Moses' absence, the Israelites prevailed upon Aaron, Moses' brother, to make them a god of gold—a calf. "Come on," they might have said, "we don't know what has happened to Moses. We need a god that will lead us out of the wilderness." The psalmist, David, wrote of those who worshiped other gods. It was a description of idol worshippers of that time, but resonates with similar people of our time:

> But their idols are silver and gold, made by human hands. They have mouths, but cannot speak, eyes, but cannot see. They have ears, but cannot hear, noses, but cannot smell. They have hands, but cannot feel, feet, but cannot walk, nor can they utter a sound with their throats. Those who make them will be like them, and so will all who trust in them. Psalm 115:4–8 NIV

While the people danced before the golden calf, God warned Moses of trouble in the camp and threatened to destroy the people Moses had led out of Egypt. Moses interceded for the rebellious Israelites, and God heeded his plea to spare them. As Joshua and Moses reached the bottom of Mount Sinai, they were stunned by the sight that met their eyes:

> When Moses approached the camp and saw the calf and the dancing, his anger burned and he threw the tablets out of his hands, breaking them to pieces at the foot of the mountain. And he took the calf the people had made and burned it in the fire; then he ground it to powder, scattered it on the water and made the Israelites drink it.
>
> Exodus 32:19–20 NIV

Moses must have turned to Aaron and asked, "What were you thinking?!" Aaron's answer would have won an Oscar for his response and his lame excuse. Can you picture him with arms upraised and a shrug of his shoulders?

"Do not be angry, my lord," Aaron might have answered. "You know how prone these people are to evil. They said to me, 'Make us gods who will go before us. As for this fellow

Moses who brought us up out of Egypt, we don't know what has happened to him.' So I told them, 'Whoever has any gold jewelry, take it off.' Then they gave me the gold, and I threw it into the fire, and *out came this calf!*"

Aaron didn't bow in contrition and take responsibility for his actions; he tried to justify going along with the crowd. How often does that still happen—drifting into disobedience instead of taking a stand? We chuckle at Aaron's disingenuous reply, but haven't we been guilty of the same? We excuse our own behavior while pointing a finger at someone else's fall into sin.

So distraught was Moses that he literally drew a line in the sand:

> So he stood at the entrance to the camp and shouted, "All of you who are on the Lord's side, come here and join me." And all the Levites gathered around him. Moses told them, "This is what the Lord, the God of Israel, says: Each of you, take your swords and go back and forth from one end of the camp to the other. Kill everyone—even your brothers, friends, and neighbors." The Levites obeyed Moses' command, and about 3,000 people died that day. Exodus 32:26–28 NLT

On the day that the Law of Moses was given, 3,000 died because of sin in the camp. After Peter's sermon on the day of Pentecost, Luke tells us in Acts 2 that 3,000 were saved because of grace.

The day of Pentecost was so much more than tongues of fire and the disciples speaking in other languages. It was a new covenant: the Holy Spirit coming to earth to dwell in God's people. The prophet Jeremiah spoke to the children of Israel:

> But this is the covenant that I will make with the house of Israel after those days, says the Lord: I will put My law in their minds, and write it on their hearts; and I will be their God, and they shall be My people. Jeremiah 31:33 NKJV

At Sinai, the law was imparted on tablets of stone; in the upper room it was written on hearts of flesh and the people of God were called to be a holy nation and a royal priesthood (see 1 Peter 2:9).

## BETWEEN PENTECOST AND THE FEAST OF TRUMPETS

Leviticus 23 provides a picture of the past, present, and future. The first four feasts—Passover, Unleavened Bread,

Firstfruits, and Pentecost—outline events that were fulfilled by Christ during His time on earth. Some Bible scholars believe the Church today is living in the three-month period between Pentecost and *Rosh Hashanah*, the Feast of Trumpets. In Leviticus 23:22 (NLT), God defined what was to take place during this time:

> "When you harvest the crops of your land, do not harvest the grain along the edges of your fields, and do not pick up what the harvesters drop. Leave it for the poor and the foreigners living among you. I am the Lord your God."

Pastor Iain Gordon again provides insight on what he calls this "sneaky" little verse:

> You can just take it as general instruction that He cares for the poor and those outside of Israel (which is certainly true) but in that all of this chapter is also prophetic in nature, I believe there is more to this verse than the obvious.
>
> I believe that God has placed this as a sneaky little verse between Passover and Trumpets because He was indicating what

He was going to do between the fulfillment of these two feasts. As you may remember from the introduction to the feasts study, between the spring and fall feasts there is a gap of over three months. Prophetically, this gap speaks of the Church age that began at Pentecost and will conclude at Trumpets. So what did God do during this time? He did [precisely] what He told Israel to do—He remembered the poor and alien (foreigner/stranger) in sending His word to the far ends of the earth so that the Gentiles could be saved. Now that age still continues today. It is the age of grace and shall continue until the day when trumpet sounds . . . and I believe we are very close to the time for the fulfilment of the feast of Trumpets to occur. Let's have a look at this exciting and important feast.[21]

# CHAPTER 6

*Then the Lord spoke to Moses, saying, "Speak to the children of Israel, saying: 'In the seventh month, on the first day of the month, you shall have a sabbath-rest, a memorial of blowing of trumpets, a holy convocation. You shall do no customary work on it; and you shall offer an offering made by fire to the Lord.'"*

LEVITICUS 23:23–25 NKJV

The first of the autumn feasts was that of the Feast of Trumpets, or *Zikhron Teruah*, and now called Rosh Hashanah. It falls on the first day of *Tishrei*, the seventh month of the Hebrew calendar, and was introduced to the Israelites in Leviticus 23:23–25 (NIV):

> The LORD said to Moses, "Say to the Israelites: 'On the first day of the seventh month you are to have a day of sabbath rest, a sacred assembly commemorated with trumpet blasts.

Do no regular work, but present a food offering to the LORD.'"

This fifth feast is followed by *Yom Kippur,* or the
Day of Atonement, and lastly by the Feast of Taberna-
cles. The usage of the term *Rosh Hashanah,* "the begin-
ning of the year," was introduced in the second century
AD after the temple and Jerusalem were razed by the
Romans.

Mention of the celebration of the Feast of Trumpets
can be found in the Old Testament and is recorded in the
companion books of Ezra (3:1–6) and Nehemiah (7:73–8:13).
The Israelites had returned from captivity in Babylon, and
the temple altar had been rebuilt. On the first day of the
seventh month, Ezra stood before the assembled people and
read from the book of the law. He concluded his reading of
the Torah with

> "This day is holy to the Lord your God; do
> not mourn nor weep." For all the people wept,
> when they heard the words of the Law. Then
> he said to them, "Go your way, eat the fat,
> drink the sweet, and send portions to those
> for whom nothing is prepared; for this day
> is holy to our Lord. Do not sorrow, for the

joy of the Lord is your strength." Nehemiah 8:9b–10 NKJV

Rosh Hashanah is set aside as a day of rest and is celebrated by intermittent trumpet blasts, followed by ten days of repentance before the High Holy Day of Yom Kippur. The writers of *Rose Guide to the Tabernacle* indicate:

> Jewish tradition says that God writes every person's words, deeds, and thoughts in the book of life, which he opens on Rosh Hashanah.... If good deeds outnumber sinful ones for the year, the person's name will be inscribed in the book of life for another year on Yom Kippur. During Rosh HaShanah and the "Ten Days of Repentance," people can repent of their sins and do good deeds to increase their chances of being inscribed in the book of life.[22]

## THE THREE FINAL FEASTS

The final three feasts of the Jewish year parallel events surrounding the coming of the Messiah as foretold in the Scriptures. The first of these is the Feast of Trumpets, accompanied by the blowing of the shofar—a musical instrument of ancient origin, traditionally made of a ram's horn, used for Jewish religious purposes.[23] The sounds heard during the Feast of Trumpets are an important ingredient in the Old and New Testaments. It is a public acknowledgment of Jehovah as King of Kings.

The first day of the feast is to be a day of rest. Although it ushers in a new year, it is not a frivolous holiday as is the world's current New Year's celebrations; instead, it is the beginning of a time of reflection and repentance. The Feast of Trumpets is followed by Yom Kippur (Day of Atonement) and then the Feast of Tabernacles.

During the Feast of Trumpets, there are specific guidelines for the way the shofar is to be blown. The sound of the ram's horn also signals the beginning of Rosh Hashanah and is a sacred appeal to the listener to contemplate his or her transgressions. There is a specific sequence for blasts on the instrument:

✧ The first sound heard is the *Tekiah*, or a long blast;

✧ Second is the *Shevarim*, or three short blasts said to mimic the playing of a trumpet. Some have said this sound resembles the cries of a man yearning to reconnect with Jehovah and believe it is the cry of a "broken spirit; a broken and contrite heart" (Psalm 51:17 NIV).

✧ The third sound is the *Teruah*. The writers on AISH.com define the call as: The Teruah sound—9 quick blasts in short succession—resembles an alarm clock, arousing us from our spiritual slumber. The shofar brings clarity, alertness, and focus.[24]

Jewish conference speaker and writer Sam Nadler gives us insight into the observance during Rosh Hashanah:

The synagogue service during Rosh Hashanah included three fundamental sections. The first section is called Malkiyot (Kingships) emphasizing the fact of God's sovereignty. The second section is called Zikhronot (Remembrance) which testifies to the fact that our God does remember His covenants and promises to Israel. The third section is the Shofarot section when the shofar is blown. Traditionally, the shofar brings to memory God's provision of the ram that Abraham sacrificed in place of his only son, Isaac.[25]

The *Mishnah* (a record of oral traditions) refers to Rosh Hashanah as the day of judgment. The volume indicates that on that particular feast day Jehovah views a series of three books. The Book of Life records the destiny of the righteous; the Book of Death records the fate of the wicked. The majority will be found in neither tome and are therefore given a ten-day grace period—until the High Holy Day of Yom Kippur—to repent before their future is sealed. The unrepentant will be "blotted out of the book of life, and not be written with the righteous" (Psalm 69:28 HNV).

On Rosh Hashanah, Jews greet each other with *Shanah Tovah*, meaning, "Have a good year." The meal enjoyed on that feast day may include apples or challah bread dipped in honey as a symbol of a sweet year to come.

## THE FEAST AND THE MESSIAH

The prophet Daniel (12:2 NIV) wrote:

Multitudes who sleep in the dust of the earth will awake: some to everlasting life, others to shame and everlasting contempt.

Matthew 24:31 (HNV) records:

> He will send out his angels with a great
> sound of a shofar, and they will gather
> together his elect from the four winds, from
> one end of the sky to the other.

Daniel foresaw the resurrection and rapture of the body of Christ. The call on the shofar was the signal to gather the children of God to meet Him in the air. Jesus reminded His disciples of the words of Daniel, and in 1 Corinthians 15:50–55 (NKJV), Paul interwove the two prophecies:

> Now this I say, brethren, that flesh and
> blood cannot inherit the kingdom of God; nor
> does corruption inherit incorruption. Behold,
> I tell you a mystery: We shall not all sleep, but
> we shall all be changed—in a moment, in the
> twinkling of an eye, at the last trumpet. For
> the trumpet will sound, and the dead will be
> raised incorruptible, and we shall be changed.
> For this corruptible must put on incorruption,
> and this mortal must put on immortality. So
> when this corruptible has put on incorrup-
> tion, and this mortal has put on immortality,

then shall be brought to pass the saying that

is written: "Death is swallowed up in victory."

O Death, where is your sting? O Hades, where

is your victory?

The sound of the trumpet will also signal a much more devastating event: the beginning of what Jeremiah the prophet identified as "the time of Jacob's trouble" (see Jeremiah 30:7). It is the time to which Jesus referred in Matthew 24:21–22 (NKJV):

For then there will be great tribulation,

such as has not been since the beginning of

the world until this time, no, nor ever shall

be. And unless those days were shortened, no

flesh would be saved; but for the elect's sake

those days will be shortened.

Just as the observers of Rosh Hashanah are called upon to examine their lives, so must believers in Jesus Christ reassess their commitment to Him, to His work, and to His Word. In 2 Peter 3:9 God reminds us that He is not willing that any of His people perish, "but that all should come to repentance" (NKJV). Believers await the sound of the trumpet as a climax of world events for those who have had the doorposts of their lives covered with the blood of the sacrificial Lamb. It is God's will and purpose to write our names in the Lamb's Book of Life, not just for a year but for all eternity. The prophet Ezekiel describes what Jehovah God wishes to offer us:

> Then I will sprinkle clean water on you, and you shall be clean; I will cleanse you from all your filthiness and from all your idols. I will give you a new heart and put a new spirit within you; I will take the heart of stone out of your flesh and give you a heart of flesh. I will put My Spirit within you and cause you to walk in My statutes, and you will keep My judgments and do them. Ezekiel 36:25–27 NKJV

The writer of Hebrews penned:

> Let us draw near with a true heart in full assurance of faith, having our hearts sprinkled from an evil conscience and our bodies washed with pure water. Let us hold fast the confession of our hope without wavering, for He who promised is faithful. Hebrews 10:22–23 NKJV

While we may laugh at the *Peanuts* cartoon character Pigpen, who is always surrounded by a cloud of dust, and chuckle over scenes of people tumbling into a mud puddle or being splashed with dirty water, it would be distasteful for most not to have a regular bath.

Yet we eschew the spiritual cleanliness of which Solomon wrote in Proverbs, and James in the New Testament:

> There are those who are clean in their own eyes but are not washed of their filth.
> Proverbs 30:12 ESV

> Draw near to God, and he will draw near to you. Cleanse your hands, you sinners, and purify your hearts, you double-minded.
> James 4:8 ESV

As we watch, work, and wait, we, like the child Jesus, must be about our heavenly Father's business (see Luke 2:49).

Jesus charged His disciples with their task in John 9:4 (NLT):

> We must quickly carry out the tasks assigned us by the one who sent us. The night is coming, and then no one can work.

Not only must we listen for the sound of the trumpet, we must take time daily to reevaluate our relationship with our Lord, *before* the trumpet sounds. Ask Him, through the *Ruach HaKodesh*—the Holy Spirit—to reveal any sin in your life, and ask for help to live the life God has called us to live in Him. His grace is sufficient in every situation and circumstance of our life.

# CHAPTER 7

*And the Lord spoke to Moses, saying: "Also the tenth day of this seventh month shall be the Day of Atonement. It shall be a holy convocation for you; you shall afflict your souls, and offer an offering made by fire to the Lord. And you shall do no work on that same day, for it is the Day of Atonement, to make atonement for you before the Lord your God. For any person who is not afflicted in soul on that same day shall be cut off from his people. And any person who does any work on that same day, that person I will destroy from among his people. You shall do no manner of work; it shall be a statute forever throughout your generations in all your dwellings. It shall be to you a sabbath of solemn rest, and you shall afflict your souls; on the ninth day of the month at evening, from evening to evening, you shall celebrate your sabbath."*

LEVITICUS 23:26–32 NKJV

Yom Kippur, or Day of Atonement, is the most sacred of all the High Holy Days celebrated by the Jews. It is a day for sober personal assessment; the only sacred assembly that requires mourning. The observance of Yom Kippur was established as a means for Jehovah to temporarily reconcile the sin problem and its devastating effects on mankind, and to restore the relationship between Jehovah and His chosen people.

The word *atonement* appears multiple times in just one chapter of Leviticus—chapter 16. Leviticus 16:1 states, "The LORD spoke to Moses after the death of the two sons of Aaron, when they drew near before the LORD and died" (ESV).

Aaron was chosen by God to serve as high priest, and the two oldest of his four sons as priests in the tabernacle. Nadab and Abihu were standing alongside Moses at the base of Mount Sinai; the brothers experienced firsthand the power, presence, and glory of Jehovah. What could Nadab and Abihu possibly have done to elicit such a strong reaction? The two men broke the laws God had established for service in the tabernacle:

- ✧ The men took on a role that was not assigned to them. Only the high priest was to offer incense in the Holy of Holies.

- ✧ They made the offering in vessels that had not been anointed with oil and set apart for service.

- ✧ Nadab and Abihu acted without the

authority of either Moses or Aaron, and certainly without the blessing of Jehovah.

✧ Their actions were driven by pride, egoism, arrogance, and self-aggrandizement. They lacked respect for authority and, more importantly, for the holiness of God.

✧ Leviticus 10:9–10 indicates that the two brothers might have been under the influence of strong drink.

✧ Incense was only to be offered annually on the Day of Atonement, and under very specific guidelines.

Following ten days of repentance after Rosh Hashanah, the Israelites were instructed to observe the Day of Atonement. The high priest was to be the earthly mediator between the Israelites and Jehovah. It was a position of the loftiest honor and his duties were sacred. On the Day of Atonement, he was to offer sacrifices for the sins of the people and make intercession before the mercy seat in the Holy of Holies.

On Yom Kippur, the high priest donned garments that would have consisted of

✧ a tunic of white linen woven in one piece

(Note: Could the seamlessly woven robe worn by Jesus at His crucifixion indicate His position as High Priest? Hebrews 4:14, says, "Therefore, since we have a great high priest who has ascended into heaven, Jesus the Son of God, let us hold firmly to the faith we profess.");

✧ a robe of dark blue, the hem decorated with purple, scarlet, and blue pomegranates;

✧ an apron or ephod woven from threads of gold, blue, purple, and scarlet;

✧ a golden girdle tied around the waist;

✧ pouches containing twelve onyx stones engraved with the names of the tribes of Israel;

✧ a breastplate made of threads of gold, blue, purple, and scarlet linen containing four rows of three jewels. Each jewel in a gold setting was engraved with the name of one of the tribes. It was held in place with rings of gold attached to the shoulder of the ephod. A pocket made into the breastplate contained the Urim and Thummim (objects used to determine God's will).

✧ a golden crown on which was written "Holy to the Lord." On the Day of Atonement the high priest was charged predominately with ministering before Jehovah in the Holy of Holies. It was the most sacred of all his obligations, for the threefold cleansing of the children of Israel rested upon his shoulders. Perhaps he knew that he was the type, the shadow, of the Messiah who was to come to redeem mankind from the burden of sin. As Jehovah had prescribed in Leviticus 16:32–33 the offering on Yom Kippur was made to bring purification, not only for the people but for the priest and his own family, as well as the temple in which the ceremony was held. [The word *atonement* is found four times in these two verses.] Moses was instructed that the high priest "is to put on the sacred linen garments and make atonement for the Most Holy Place." (Jesus, our High Priest, had a crown of thorns placed upon His head—a crown of suffering, a crown of rejection. Now He sits on the right hand of God crowned with glory and honor.) (See Hebrews 2:5–9)

## CONTEMPLATION AND REPENTANCE

Yom Kippur is the day dedicated to the contemplation of one's past sins. The people were to consider from what they had been delivered—the bondage of the Egyptians. On that day, the high priest was to make the designated sacrifices—two goats and a ram for the Israelites and a bull and ram for himself and his household. The animals were to be without spot or blemish according to the Mosaic law in Leviticus 4.

The high priest was the only individual allowed to enter the Holy of Holies, and only once each year on Yom Kippur, the Day of Atonement. The curtain divided the priests who performed the daily activities in the Holy Place from the Holy of Holies. It was a barrier so that man would not casually, rashly, or disrespectfully enter into the presence of El Hakkadosh—the Holy God—who could not tolerate sin. Habakkuk 1:13 says of Jehovah, "Your eyes are too pure to look on evil; you cannot tolerate wrong-doing" (NIV).

Although specially chosen to minister in the Holy of Holies, there were exact steps that had to be undertaken by the high priest before he could safely step through the veil into the overwhelming presence of God. Once inside the veil, the high priest stood before the only item in the chamber: the ark of the covenant.

The lid of the ark was known as the "atonement cover," or the mercy seat. It held two cherubim, one at each end, fashioned from pure gold, wings outspread and meeting at the center of the cover. It symbolized God's seat of authority and His presence in the tabernacle. It was Jehovah's meeting place with the high priest as stated in Exodus 25:22: "There, above the cover between the two cherubim that are over the ark of the covenant law, I will meet with you and give you all my commands for the Israelites" (NIV).

Some Bible scholars believe there is a correlation between the lid for the ark of the covenant and the positioning of the two angels in the tomb following the resurrection of Jesus: "And she [Mary Magdalene] saw two angels in white, sitting where the body of Jesus had lain, one at the head and one at the feet (John 20:12 ESV).

In 1828, Anglican minister and poet Hugh Stowell wrote:

From every stormy wind that blows,
From every swelling tide of woes,
There is a calm, a sure retreat;
'Tis found beneath the mercy seat.

There is a place where Jesus sheds
The oil of gladness on our heads;

A place than all besides more sweet;

It is the blood bought mercy seat.[26]

The mercy seat is a place of grace; more so now because sinners can boldly approach the throne of God due to the shed blood of Jesus Christ, the ultimate sacrifice of atonement for sin.

# CHAPTER 8

*"They shall make an ark of acacia wood. Two cubits and a half shall be its length, a cubit and a half its breadth, and a cubit and a half its height. You shall overlay it with pure gold, inside and outside shall you overlay it, and you shall make on it a molding of gold around it."You shall make a mercy seat of pure gold. Two cubits and a half shall be its length, and a cubit and a half its breadth. And you shall make two cherubim of gold; of hammered work shall you make them, on the two ends of the mercy seat. Make one cherub on the one end, and one cherub on the other end. Of one piece with the mercy seat shall you make the cherubim on its two ends. The cherubim shall spread out their wings above, overshadowing the mercy seat with their wings, their faces one to another; toward the mercy seat shall the faces of the cherubim be. And you shall put the mercy seat on the top of the ark . . . "*

EXODUS 25:10–11, 17–21 ESV

A lthough it occupied the innermost chamber of the tabernacle, the ark was the first piece assembled after Moses was given the plans for the structure and its furnishings. Before approaching the veil, the high priest had washed himself and donned the clothing indicated by Jehovah for the mission.

Moses had been instructed in Leviticus 16:2, "Tell your brother Aaron that he is not to come whenever he chooses into the Most Holy Place behind the curtain in front of the atonement cover on the ark, or else he will die. For I will appear in the cloud over the atonement cover" (NIV).

Only once a year was the high priest to enter the Holy of Holies. He would carry a censer filled with coals from the altar of incense in the Holy Place and a golden bowl containing two handfuls of incense, which, once inside the Holy of Holies, was sprinkled on the burning coals. As the thick, sweet-smelling fragrance from the incense rose before the ark of the covenant, the vision of the high priest was obscured by the smoke to forestall any possibility that he might look upon God. The smoke represented the prayers of the children of Israel wafting upward on the most holy of days—the Day of Atonement.

As part of the ritual of humbling himself, the high priest would then enter the Holy Place, where he would exchange his priestly robes for the simple linen garments of an ordinary priest. The high priest was then required to painstakingly follow the rules laid down by Jehovah—on threat of death.

He was to wash himself in the Molten Sea—the brass laver—before slitting the throat of a bullock in preparation to offer its blood in the Holy of Holies.

Leviticus 16:21 (NKJV) gives the reader more insight on the role of Aaron, the high priest:

> Aaron shall lay both his hands on the head of the live goat, confess over it all the iniquities of the children of Israel, and all their transgressions, concerning all their sins, putting them on the head of the goat, and shall send it away into the wilderness by the hand of a suitable man.

The mention of iniquities, transgressions, and sins in this verse is very specific. *Sin* means to "miss the mark." The apostle Paul tells us in Romans 3:23 that it is the generalized term for anyone who falls "short of the glory of God." James 4:17 defines sin: "So whoever knows the right thing to do and fails to do it, for him it is sin" (ESV).

Iniquity is more deep-seated; it is a premeditated choice. Rather than walk the straight path, the iniquitous man deliberately chooses the crooked path. Micah 2:1 (NKJV) warns:

Woe to those who devise iniquity, and
work out evil on their beds! At morning light
they practice it, because it is in the power of
their hand.

An example would be David's liaison with Bathsheba.
The planning that led to the death of Uriah, her husband,
was well thought out by David. When the king fell on his face
before God in repentance, he cried, "Wash me thoroughly
from my iniquity, and cleanse me from my sin!" (Psalm
51:2 ESV)

Transgressions are presumptuous sins—intentional,
willful disobedience. Samson committed such sin when he
transgressed the laws of God in his dalliance with Delilah
and revealed the secret of his strength—his vow not to cut
his hair. David gave us hope in Psalm 32:1 when he wrote,
"Blessed *is he whose* transgression *is* forgiven, *Whose* sin *is*
covered" (NKJV).

In an article entitled, "What is the difference between
iniquity, sin, and transgression?" the author penned:

The biblical writers used different words
to refer to sin in its many forms. However,
regardless of how depraved a human heart
may become, Jesus' death on the cross was

sufficient to cover all sin (John 1:29; Romans 5:18). Psalm 32:5, quoted at the beginning of this article, ends with these words: "And you forgave the guilt of my sin." The only sin that God cannot forgive is the final rejection of the Holy Spirit's drawing to repentance—the ultimate fruit of a reprobate mind (Matthew 12:32; Luke 12:10).[27]

## WHY BLOOD SACRIFICES?

Why is blood, the life's force, so crucial in the sacrificial order instituted by Jehovah for forgiveness of sin? After Adam and Eve sinned in the garden of Eden, God sacrificed animals to cover their nakedness. In Genesis 4:4, righteous Abel offered a pleasing sacrifice to Jehovah. Leviticus 17:11(ESV) reveals the efficacy of blood:

> For the life of the flesh is in the blood, and I have given it for you on the altar to make atonement for your souls, for it is the blood that makes atonement by the life.

The shedding of blood became a living picture of the awfulness of sin and its dire consequences—death. Perhaps the apostle Paul gave the most vivid illustration in Romans 6:23 when he said, "For the wages of sin is death" (ESV).

After collecting the blood of the sacrificial animal in the basin, the high priest would then take up incense from the altar in his left hand, while with his right he lifted the censer of live coals. Entering the Holy of Holies, the high priest would set the censer down and take incense from the tray to sprinkle on the hot coals. The rising cloud was symbolic of the glory of God that had filled both the tabernacle and the temple when it was consecrated to Jehovah.

Leaving the Holy of Holies, the high priest would again take up the basin of blood from the bull and with his fingers sprinkle it once eastward toward the mercy seat and toward the people who waited outside the temple, and seven times on the ark of the covenant. That ceremony was followed by the sacrifice of a goat, after which the high priest would return to the Holy of Holies to sprinkle the goat's blood in the same manner. The difference was the manner in which the goat sacrificed was chosen.

## THE AZAZEL

The high priest was responsible not only for choosing the goat that was to be sacrificed but also the one to be sent away into the desert. The two animals were brought, along with an urn containing two gold coins. On one coin was written "for the people" and on the other *"azazel,"* meaning "to go away." The animals were placed on the left and right sides of the high priest and a coin was laid on the head of each. The one designated azazel had a red thread tied to its horn; the other was slain by the high priest. Once the blood of the first goat had been sprinkled in the Holy of Holies, the priest would exit into the Holy Place and anoint it as well.

David E. Lister of Moriel Ministries said of the two animals:

> Here...we see a picture of our Lord. In the bull it is the strong dying for the weak; in the goat we see the innocent dying for the guilty. While the two goats constitute one offering, I see two aspects: first with the goat that "goes away" I see Barabbas or even me. Jesus took my sin; I got to go free. But I also see the good news: the sins of the people being carried away not to be seen again. "As far as the east is from the west, so far has He removed our transgressions from us." [Psalm 103:12] Oh what a wonderful picture of how Jesus would take our sin away![28]

The last act of the high priest on Yom Kippur was to replace the linen clothing with his robes of office. He would then return to the bronze altar and offer two sacrificial rams—one for himself and one for the people, according to the Mosaic laws in Leviticus 4 and 8. The high priest was subject to death if he did not carry out his duties as instructed—an indication of the gravity of his charge. While this was being done, the people stood outside the temple waiting for the azazel to be released to carry their sins into the wilderness, not to be forgiven, but to be postponed for another year.

They must have wondered: *Has the offering been accepted? Is the high priest counted worthy to represent the people? Has he been slain by Jehovah in the Holy of Holies?* Perhaps they listened closely for the tinkle of the bells on his robe that would indicate he had safely returned to the Holy Place.

Author Sam Nadler wrote of sin and sacrifice:

> Yom Kippur reminds us that we are fallen creatures resting only in the grace, mercy, and atonement of God in Messiah. Works apart from Messiah are self-oriented activities which are mere efforts to prove what we can

do. Biblical humility is essential to restoring relationships. Only through this humility we can apply and enjoy the benefits of forgiveness in the atonement made in Messiah.[29]

A look at Hebrews 7:23–28 (NIV) gives us a picture of the perfect work of Jesus Christ on the cross:

> Now there have been many of those priests, since death prevented them from continuing in office; but because Jesus lives forever, he has a permanent priesthood. Therefore he is able to save completely those who come to God through him, because he always lives to intercede for them. Such a high priest truly meets our need—one who is holy, blameless, pure, set apart from sinners, exalted above the heavens. Unlike the other high priests, he does not need to offer sacrifices day after day, first for his own sins, and then for the sins of the people. He sacrificed for their sins once for all when he offered himself. For the law appoints as high priests men in all their weakness; but the oath, which came after the

law, appointed the Son, who has been made perfect forever.

## CAIN AND ABEL—THE STORY OF SIN AND SACRIFICE

The story of Cain and Abel in Genesis is one of an acceptable sacrifice for sin as opposed to a casual treatment of the rift in man's relationship with God. Although the sacrifice by God in the garden was the first shedding of blood, it would surely not be the last sacrifice offered. One of the earliest examples of an acceptable sacrifice to Jehovah was that of Abel, the second son of Adam and Eve. In Hebrew, Abel means "breath, or vapor," perhaps an indication of the shortness of his life. James wrote: "Your life is like the morning fog—it's here a little while, then it's gone" (James 4:14 NLT).

Cain, the older brother, was a tiller of the ground—a farmer; Abel was a shepherd. Genesis does not tell us exactly how the two brothers knew what was considered a proper sacrifice to the most Holy God, but clearly they did.

The story of God's grace to their parents must have been told over and over to Cain and Abel. Both worshiped God and brought sacrifices to present to Him—but each brought a different offering. Genesis 4:3 tells us that "Cain brought...

the fruit of the ground" (NKJV). He approached the altar of sacrifice with whatever he could pluck from his garden. His gift was one of convenience—for show, one given not in faith, but in haste, a last-minute effort. Though he gave lip service to Jehovah, he was not a godly man; instead, he was quick to anger, self-indulgent, and jealous. Cain's wrathful response when God rejected his spur-of-the-moment offering was indicative of his character:

> But [the Lord] did not accept Cain and his gift. This made Cain very angry, and he looked dejected. "Why are you so angry?" the Lord asked Cain. "Why do you look so dejected?" Genesis 4:5–6 NLT

Cain was angry that God dared to reject his sacrifice. He was so indignant that he stood boldly at the altar and argued with the Creator of the universe. His anger coupled with his appalling attitude could not mask his realization that Jehovah's requirements had not been met. Even before Christ offered grace to everyone through His death on the cross, God offered Cain a second chance:

> "You will be accepted if you do what is right. But if you refuse to do what is right,

then watch out! Sin is crouching at the door, eager to control you. But you must subdue it and be its master." Genesis 4:7 NLT

Cain could have reviewed the requirements for an acceptable offering, humbled himself before God, and returned with a proper sacrifice. Instead, his choice was to stomp angrily away with Jehovah's warning ringing in his ears. Sin became his master and he responded accordingly.

Abel had made preparation for his offering by choosing a firstborn from his flock. He did not choose a skinny, lame, marred lamb; rather, it was the best he had to offer. Abel approached the altar humbly and penitently, bowed low in the presence of Almighty God, and presented his gift with faith that his obedience would be honored—his gift accepted.

Abel's offering of a sheep was his way of acknowledging what God had done in the garden when He wrapped Abel's mother and father in animal skins. He presented an animal from his flock as both a thank offering and a sin offering. In essence, he was saying, "I want to be obedient. I am thanking You for showing grace to my parents, and I am asking You to show the same grace to me."

The two brothers walked away from the altar with totally different countenances. Abel's was radiant with God's love and approval; Cain's was dark, his face infused with rage, his heart filled with jealousy and murderous intent.

Noted Christian pastor, author, and teacher Charles Swindoll wrote of jealousy:

> This was Cain's sin. He was jealous of Abel. He resented God's acceptance of his brother. No doubt his face was red with emotion and his eyes filled with rage as God smiled on Abel's sacrifice. Not until Abel's warm blood poured over Cain's cruel hands did jealousy subside.[30]

Solomon, the wise king, defined the effects of such jealousy when he wrote, "Jealousy is fierce as the grave. Its flashes are flashes of fire" (Song of Solomon 8:6 ESV).

Abel's hands were raised in praise to Jehovah; Cain's fists were clenched in fury. He was so filled with resentment that he lured his brother into the field and murdered him. Suddenly God called to Cain, "Where is Abel, your brother?"

A sullen Cain replied, "I don't have any idea. Why are you asking me, anyway? Am I my brother's keeper?" (Genesis 4:9, paraphrased.) The punishment for Cain's crime was swift and severe. God stripped him of the land that he had tilled and banished Cain from His presence. He was thrust out of

Eden and consigned to be a vagrant and wanderer. And God warned: "Therefore, whoever kills Cain, vengeance shall be taken on him sevenfold." And the LORD set a mark on Cain, lest anyone finding him should kill him (Genesis 4:15 NKJV).

When the horror of Cain's sin gripped him, he cried, "My punishment is greater than I can bear!" (Genesis 4:13 NKJV)

Of the lives of Cain and Abel, noted Christian minister and author John MacArthur wrote:

> Abel's sacrifice was accepted because he knew what God wanted and obeyed. Cain's was rejected because he knew what God wanted, yet disobeyed. To obey is righteous; to disobey is evil. Abel was of God; Cain was of Satan (1 John 3:12). . . Abel offered a better sacrifice because it represented the obedience of faith. He willingly brought God what He asked, and he brought the very best that he had. In Abel's sacrifice, the way of the cross was first [foreshadowed]. The first sacrifice was Abel's lamb—one lamb for one person. Later came the Passover [Pesach]—with one lamb for one family. Then came the Day of Atonement— with one lamb for one nation. Finally came Good Friday—one Lamb for the whole world.[31]

Jesus offered one sacrifice, Himself, and established the plan of forgiveness and reconciliation one time for all time! He laid aside his robes of glory and donned a robe of flesh so that we might have access to God, the Father. We read in 2 Corinthians 5:21, "For our sake he made him to be sin who knew no sin, so that in him we might become the righteousness of God" (ESV).

Blood-bought, forgiven, redeemed, and delivered! Believers are not saved by the character of the Sacrifice. Salvation only comes through the shed blood of Christ—the one-time-for-all-time price of atonement. Zechariah foretold the efficacy of the sacrifice of Messiah:

> Then I will pour out a spirit of grace and prayer on the house of David and the residents of Jerusalem, and they will look at Me whom they pierced. They will mourn for Him as one mourns for an only child and weep bitterly for Him as one weeps for a firstborn. Zechariah 12:10 HCSB

> On that day a fountain will be opened to the house of David and the inhabitants of Jerusalem, to cleanse them from sin and impurity. Zechariah 13:1 NIV

The words of an old song written by Fanny Crosby ring with praise:

> Redeemed, how I love to proclaim it!
>
> Redeemed by the blood of the Lamb;
>
> Redeemed through His infinite mercy,
>
> His child and forever I am.[32]

The Day of Atonement ends with the blowing of the shofar. One day the blowing of the trumpet will resound through the heavens and God, the Father, will declare that time is no more. The prophet Joel prophesied that great day:

> Blow the trumpet in Zion,
>
> And sound an alarm in My holy mountain!
>
> Let all the inhabitants of the land tremble;
>
> For the day of the Lord is coming,
>
> For it is at hand. Joel 2:1 NKJV

Christ is waiting to present, "a glorious church, not having spot, or wrinkle, or any such thing; but that it should be holy and without blemish" (Ephesians 5:27 KJV).

# CHAPTER 9

*"Also on the fifteenth day of the seventh month, when you have
gathered in the fruit of the land, you shall keep the feast of the
Lord for seven days; on the first day there shall be a sabbath-
rest, and on the eighth day a sabbath-rest. And you shall take for
yourselves on the first day the fruit of beautiful trees, branches of
palm trees, the boughs of leafy trees, and willows of the brook; and
you shall rejoice before the Lord your God for seven days. You shall
keep it as a feast to the Lord for seven days in the year. It shall be
a statute forever in your generations. You shall celebrate it in the
seventh month. You shall dwell in booths for seven days. All who
are native Israelites shall dwell in booths, that your generations
may know that I made the children of Israel dwell in booths when
I brought them out of the land of Egypt: I am the Lord your God."*

LEVITICUS 23:39-43 NKJV

Following the Day of Atonement is *Sukkot*, the Feast of
Tabernacles, or Booths. It is a celebration of the fall
harvest, which even today lasts an entire week. The Israelites
built temporary dwellings as a reminder of their forty-year
trek through the wilderness. Jews today quickly construct a

small hut where meals are eaten during the festival. Leviticus 23:40 (NIV) detailed the materials to be used: "On the first day you are to take branches from luxuriant trees—from palms, willows and other leafy trees—and rejoice before the LORD your God for seven days." The branches used to build the booths were symbolic of victory (palm), peace (olive), and willow (blessings). The *sukkah*, or shelter, must have at least three walls with a roof of branches to allow rain to fall inside. It is usually decorated with flowers and fruit, and one must also be able to view the stars.

The feast is commemorated for eight days in the land of Israel, and nine days wherever Jews are scattered worldwide. On the first day of the observance and the final day, no manual labor is permitted. During the interim, a period called *Chol Ha-Mo'ed*, work is allowed.

The Feast of Tabernacles is a feast of expectation; an ancient reminder that one day the children of Israel would be firmly planted in their own land looking forward with anticipation to the arrival of the Messiah. It is also a time to remember Jehovah's blessings. It is a time of restored communion with God, and a reminder that this sojourn on earth is only temporary. In ancient days, the Feast of Tabernacles was so festive that it was often referred to simply as "The Feast."

From a sacred viewpoint, the feast is a celebration of the joy of knowing that for another year one's sins will be forgiven. From a prophetic outlook, it is a look forward to the coming of Yeshua after which, according to Zechariah 14:16, "Then the survivors from all the nations that have attacked Jerusalem will go up year after year to worship the King, the LORD Almighty, and to celebrate the Festival of Tabernacles" (NIV).

## THE JOY OF SUKKOT

Sukkot is a time of great happiness, of parties, of praise, of hospitality. The Shabbat that occurs during the feast is a time to read the Torah, especially the book of Ecclesiastes (symbolic of the reality that life is fleeting). On the evening at the beginning of the feast, candles are lit just before the sun sets and blessings are recited. After sundown, a prayer of thanksgiving is offered. Before the evening meal, *Kiddush* (a blessing recited over wine or grape juice) is recited, or perhaps only a shortened version of the blessing of the wine. This is followed by the Sukkah blessing and then the blessing of the bread. The *lulav* is waved. It is a closed frond from the date palm, and is a part of "the Four Species used during the Jewish holiday of Sukkot. The other [three] are the *hadass* (myrtle), *aravah* (willow), and *etrog* (citron)."[33] Songs of praise are sung, usually taken from Psalm 136: "Give thanks to the LORD, for he is good, for his steadfast love endures forever" (v. 1 ESV). The family and friends then move into the Sukkah to pray together, eat, enjoy music, and generally unwind.

In Old Testament times, it was also a time of sacrifice. In his book *Thus Shalt Thou Serve: The Feasts and Offerings of Ancient Israel*, author and Bible teacher C. W. Slemming wrote:

> Numbers 29 lists the number of animals to be used in the sacrifices of that week. The young bulls, diminishing in number from day to day for eight days, were 13, 12, 11, 10, 9, 8, 7, 1. It has been suggested that the decrease to the one foretells...how the many sacrifices of the law would, in the fullness of time, be reduced to the One Sacrifice that would be made once in the end of the age . . . . On the last day of the feast there were special celebrations and joy.[34]

In John 7:37, we read that Jesus went up to Jerusalem during this particular feast. While there, He declared, "Let anyone who is thirsty come to me and drink" (NIV).

Of this declaration, Slemming wrote:

> Thus the Lord was turning the thoughts
> of the people away from the shadow to the
> substance, away from ritual to reality.[35]

The feasts were times when all physically able Jewish males were charged with going up to Jerusalem to appear before the Lord in the temple, the place that was symbolic of His presence. There they called to remembrance what Jehovah had done in bringing them out of Egypt into the Promised Land. They praised God for His provision and offered up sacrifices that would postpone their sins for another year.

> But when the fullness of time had come,
> God sent forth his Son, born of woman, born
> under the law, to redeem those who were
> under the law, so that we might receive adop-
> tion as sons. Galatians 4:4–5 ESV

## SUKKOT AND PROPHECY

There are several prophetic dimensions associated with Sukkot. As we saw in Zechariah 16, it is an image of the time when the world will worship the Messiah in Jerusalem. Just as it was a remembrance of the time that God sheltered the Israelites in a cloud by day and a pillar of fire by night, it is a vision of the time when Israel will no longer be oppressed by ungodly nations. Ezekiel 37:26–27 (NKJV) gives us a preview of Israel's future:

> Moreover I will make a covenant of peace with them, and it shall be an everlasting covenant with them; I will establish them and multiply them, and I will set My sanctuary in their midst forevermore. My tabernacle also shall be with them; indeed I will be their God, and they shall be My people.

There were two ceremonies observed on the last day of the feast. In the first, water was carried by a priest from the Pool of Siloam to the temple. It was symbolic of the coming of the Messiah when, according to Isaiah 11:9, "For the earth shall be full of the knowledge of the LORD as the waters cover the sea" (NKJV). The people also marched around the temple carrying torches evocative of the Messiah who would be the light of the world.

Jesus was in Jerusalem with His disciples on the last day of the feast. The New Testament gives us a glimpse into Jesus' last observance of those two practices:

On the last day, that great day of the feast, Jesus stood and cried out, saying, "If anyone thirsts, let him come to Me and drink. He who believes in Me, as the Scripture has said, out of his heart will flow rivers of living water." John 7:37–38 NKJV

Then Jesus spoke to them again, saying, "I am the light of the world. He who follows Me shall not walk in darkness, but have the light of life." John 8:12 NKJV

Today, the Jewish people await the coming of Mashiach, the anointed one; the Church awaits the return of Lord Yeshua who will come to tabernacle with His people. John, the Revelator, wrote:

I heard a loud shout from the throne, saying, "Look, God's home is now among his people! He will live with them, and they will be his people. God himself will be with them." Revelation 21:3 NLT

When that day appears, we will not only tabernacle with Him, we will know Him and abide with Him throughout all eternity. Our greatest joy is yet to come. David reminded us in Psalm 30:5 that "joy comes in the morning" (ESV). Jesus is coming soon for His bride. Our Lord warned in Matthew 24:44, "Therefore you also must be ready, for the Son of Man is coming at an hour you do not expect" (ESV).

> And I [John] heard a loud voice from the throne saying, "Behold, the dwelling place of God is with man. He will dwell with them, and they will be his people, and God himself will be with them as their God." Revelation 21:3 ESV

# PART II

## JESUS IN THE FEASTS: PASSION WEEK

# INTRODUCTION

Three feasts established by the old covenant given at Mount Sinai played a pivotal role in the crucifixion and resurrection of Jesus Christ, the Messiah: Passover, Firstfruits, and Unleavened Bread. They were observed within an eight-day period. During the time of Christ, they were acknowledged either as Passover or as the Feast of Unleavened Bread. In the next few chapters, we will examine how each of these celebrations, and finally the Feast of Pentecost, are the fulfillment of ancient prophecies concerning the Messiah.

God's plan was written before the foundation of the world—before Genesis 1:1 ever became a recorded reality. In six days the Master of the Universe created all that we see around us today—the heavens, the earth, the seas, animals, and man. It took the renowned Florentine artist Buonarotti four years to recreate paintings of God's works. We know him better as Michelangelo, and his artistry adorns the ceiling of the Sistine Chapel in the Vatican.

In the spring of 1508, the sculptor-turned-reluctant painter signed a contract with Pope Julius II. His mission: to embellish the ceiling of the papal chapel. His original charge was to recreate the earthly ministry of Christ, but Michelangelo had a different image of what should be done to the 134-feet long and 43-feet wide upper surface of the sanctuary. His vision was to capture the wonder of creation, the devastation of the fall of man, and God's promise of restoration through a Savior.

Day by day, the scenes unfolded. Each morning, the edges of the painted plaster laid the day before had to be scraped away before new plaster could be added. After four long, exhausting years of bringing pictures and images to fruition, Michelangelo folded his canvases, removed the scaffolding, and threw open the doors of the chapel. The light revealed a sight that has proved to be a visual delight for the over 500 years since the unveiling on October 31, 1512.

Three millennia before Michelangelo Buonarotti climbed the ladder to the ceiling of the Sistine Chapel to paint a history for all mankind, God's story of deliverance was painted with the blood of a perfect lamb on the doorposts of the houses of children of Israel in the hot desert of Egypt. Just before the exodus became a reality, He whispered into the ear of His servant, Moses, "And when I see the blood, I will pass over you" (Exodus 12:13 NKJV). The celebration of the redemption of His people came to be known as Passover. It took another fourteen hundred years for God to complete His plan that began at Passover.

The final eight days of the life of Jesus Christ were the culmination of that plan to save the lost. It was a period of time that would change the world forever, and it was accomplished through the sacrifice of another Lamb—the perfect Lamb of God. As the scenes unfolded, rage engulfed the very people Christ had come to redeem; angels stood in silence as the beloved Son of God was viciously crucified; demons rejoiced at His death. After three days bereft of hope, His disciples discovered that the stone before the tomb holding His earthly body had been rolled away. The joyous announcement was made, "He is not here, for he has risen, as he said" (Matthew 28:6 ESV). It was a morning that would forever change the world and give hope to all who believe in Him.

# CHAPTER 10

*"For the Lord GOD will help Me; therefore I will
not be disgraced; therefore I have set My face like
a flint, and I know that I will not be ashamed."*

ISAIAH 50:7 NKJV

The time had finally come for Jesus to make His way to Jerusalem. Luke 9:51 (NKJV) tells us that He "steadfastly set His face to go to Jerusalem." Luke could have just as readily echoed the verse found in Isaiah 50:7 (NLT): "Therefore, I have set my face like a stone, determined to do his will."

Three of the holy days so significant to the Jews—the feasts of Passover, Firstfruits, and Unleavened Bread—fell within an eight-day period whose dates were contingent on the lunar calendar. Luke 22:7 refers to this time as "the day of Unleavened Bread," while John simply calls it the week of "the Passover." The feasts were all dictated by Mosaic law as set forth in Exodus, Leviticus, and Numbers. What is now often referred to as Passion Week began on Sunday, the tenth of Nisan. In John 12:1 (NLT), the disciple started the countdown to the most horrific event in the life of Christ, yet the most gratifying for Believers:

Six days before the Passover celebration began, Jesus arrived in Bethany, the home of Lazarus—the man he had raised from the dead.

The following morning Jesus and His disciples set out for Jerusalem. It was on that particular day that the lambs were culled from the flocks in the fields near Bethlehem. They were then driven to Jerusalem, through the Sheep Gate, and readied for Passover selection. The lambs were chosen on the ninth day of Nisan so that they could be safely inside the family's home by sundown, the beginning of the tenth day of Nisan. Passover would be celebrated on the fourteenth day.

On that morning, Jesus dispatched two of His disciples to Bethphage on a very specific mission:

"Go to the village ahead of you, and at once you will find a donkey tied there, with her colt by her. Untie them and bring them to

me. If anyone says anything to you, say that
the Lord needs them, and he will send them
right away." This took place to fulfill what was
spoken through the prophet: "Say to Daughter
Zion, 'See, your king comes to you, gentle and
riding on a donkey, and on a colt, the foal of a
donkey.'" Matthew 21:2–5 NIV

Jerusalem was overrun with crowds of people who had
amassed to celebrate the Feast of Passover. Women were
busy preparing for the Seder—the meal that, true to this
day, symbolizes the deliverance of the Jews from slavery in
Egypt. Yearly, they prayed that God would send the Messiah to rescue His people from Roman tyranny. So Jesus'
instructions were fulfilled and a donkey was brought to
Him. The disciples had removed their cloaks to pad the bony
back of the colt, fashioning a makeshift saddle by layering
their coats. Jesus climbed astride and began His ride into
Jerusalem—a city whose ranks had swelled for Passover by
several thousand celebrants.

Biblical scholar Alfred Edersheim wrote of Jesus' entry
into Jerusalem:

Immediately before was the Valley of the
Kedron, here seen in its greatest depth as it

joins the Valley of Hinnom, and thus giving full effect to the great peculiarity of Jerusalem, seen only on its eastern side—its situation as of a City rising out of a deep abyss. It is hardly possible to doubt that this rise and turn of the road—this rocky ledge—was the exact point where the multitude paused again, and "He, when He beheld the City, wept over it." Not with still weeping (εδακρυσεν), as at the grave of Lazarus, but with loud and deep lamentation (εκλαυσεν). The contrast was, indeed, terrible between the Jerusalem that rose before Him in all its beauty, glory, and security, and the Jerusalem which He saw in vision dimly rising on the sky, with the camp of the enemy around about it on every side, hugging it closer and closer in deadly embrace, and the very 'stockade' which the Roman Legions raised around it; then, another scene in the shifting panorama, and the city laid with the ground, and the gory bodies of her children among her ruins; and yet another scene: the silence and desolateness of death by the Hand of God—not one stone left upon another![36]

The gates of Jerusalem had seen the entry of a number of kings: massive entourages, heralds with trumpets, numerous guards and soldiers armed with swords and marching in step. This was customary and was designed to intimidate those about to be taken into captivity. Jesus was a different kind of king. He came not to dominate with power, but to serve in humility. He entered the city, not on a magnificent white stallion signifying war, but on a donkey—a mark of humility, of meekness.

Jesus was welcomed with the sound of waving palm branches, the swish muffled by the shouts of "Hosanna to the Son of David!" "Blessed is he who comes in the name of the Lord!" "Hosanna in the highest heaven!" (Matthew 21:9). Of course, the Pharisees chided Jesus and His followers and called for Him to "rebuke your disciples." Jesus replied that if the people were silenced, the very stones would cry out (see Luke 19).

Chuck Warnock, pastor of Chatham Baptist Church, wrote of the triumphal entry:

> They have been looking for a hero, and Jesus is the flavor of the day. And, of course, there were strange reports that he could heal people, feed people, and that when he prayed

evil spirits fled from those they possessed. All the more reason to admire Jesus—he was both a revolutionary and a mystic. A great combination for the nation.

But the problem with admirers is that they see what they want to see in their hero of the day. What the crowds saw in Jesus was the son of Joseph, not the Son of God. They saw him as a revolutionary, not as Redeemer. They wanted another Maccabee, not a new Messiah. In short, they admired Jesus because they thought he was the answer to all their problems.[37]

## PASSOVER IN JERUSALEM

The reception Jesus received was not a precursor to a hero being crowned king of Israel as the people intended; it was instead preparation for Jesus' death on the cross. He didn't need the adulation of the crowd to determine who He was. He knew without question that He was the Son of God, the Messiah, the red thread of salvation that runs through the pages of scripture from Genesis to Revelation. Jesus was a different kind of monarch. He knew that at the end of His mission, He would mount not a throne but a cross. Now He must make a statement bold enough to force the hand of the high priest and the Sanhedrin—the time had come.

Teddy Kollek and Moshe Pearlman wrote of Jesus' decision to go to Jerusalem for Passover:

> By the time he [Jesus] came to Jerusalem on what was to be his last Passover, he was already well known—and marked as a dangerous rebel. He was aware of the threat to his life if he forsook the comparative safety of Galilee and made this pilgrimage, when Jerusalem would be thronged with visitors and the Romans would be on the alert for revolt.[38]

What better way to provoke both the Romans and the Jewish leaders than for the people to proclaim Him "King of the Jews." Heretofore, He had stayed in the background, trying as much as possible to avoid large gatherings and the accompanying publicity. This day was different; this day was a declaration of His purpose—to fulfill the Old Testament prophecies regarding the Messiah that was to come.

In John 10:18 (NLT), Jesus said:

No one can take my life from me. I sacrifice it voluntarily. For I have the authority to lay it down when I want to and also to take it up again. For this is what my Father has commanded.

With that knowledge, He chose the day of revelation. Jesus chose the method by which He would make himself known. He chose the day His fate would be sealed and humbly offered His life. He was well aware of the outcome of His choice—death!

# CHAPTER 11

*The next day as they were leaving Bethany, Jesus was
hungry. Seeing in the distance a fig tree in leaf, he went to find
out if it had any fruit. When he reached it, he found nothing but
leaves, because it was not the season for figs. Then he said to
the tree, "May no one ever eat fruit from you again." And his
disciples heard him say it. On reaching Jerusalem, Jesus entered
the temple courts and began driving out those who were buying
and selling there. He overturned the tables of the money changers
and the benches of those selling doves, and would not allow
anyone to carry merchandise through the temple courts. And
as he taught them, he said, "Is it not written: 'My house will be
called a house of prayer for all nations'? But you have made it
'a den of robbers.'" The chief priests and the teachers of the law
heard this and began looking for a way to kill him, for they feared
him, because the whole crowd was amazed at his teaching.*

MARK 11:12–18 NIV

Monday morning, at the beginning of Holy Week, Jesus
had been ushered into Jerusalem sitting on a donkey
and amid shouts of "Hosanna." The noise of the crowd had
resembled the sound of thunder as it rolled across the city
from the Eastern Gate to the Temple Mount.

Matthew 21:12–13 (ESV) relates what happened when they arrived:

> And Jesus entered the temple and drove
> out all who sold and bought in the temple,
> and he overturned the tables of the money-
> changers and the seats of those who sold
> pigeons. He said to them, "It is written, 'My
> house shall be called a house of prayer,' but
> you make it a den of robbers."

What prompted Jesus to make such an uncompromising statement? He was in Jerusalem for Passover, the most sacred of all Jewish feasts. It was the time in the celebration, just before the Seder, when all Hebrew women cleansed their homes from any trace of leaven, a symbol of sin. Jesus looked about with what must have been great dismay; His Father's house was rife with the greediness of the money changers and merchants who had taken up residence in the temple court. Dr. John MacArthur, pastor and theologian, wrote:

> What had begun as a service to the wor-
> shipers had, under the corrupt rule of the
> chief priests, degenerated into exploitation
> and usury. Religion had become external,

crass, and materialistic; the temple of God had become a "robbers' den" (Matt. 21:13).

As He surveyed the sacred temple grounds now turned into a bazaar, Jesus was appalled and outraged. The worshipful atmosphere that befitted the temple, as the symbol of God's presence, was completely absent. What should have been a place of sacred reverence and adoration had become a place of abusive commerce and excessive overpricing. The sound of heartfelt praise and fervent prayers had been drowned out by the bawling of oxen, the bleating of sheep, the cooing of doves, and the loud haggling of vendors and their customers.[39]

No longer was Jehovah at the center of temple worship; a disease had taken center stage in God's house: the cancer of greed. As the Jews from Roman and Greek regions filed into Jerusalem to celebrate Passover, a temple tax was demanded. The only currency acceptable to the priests was the shekel, which was coined in Israel. It was open season for money changers who would take the foreign currency and, for a fee, exchange it for the customary shekel.

Then there were the animal vendors who were there, ostensibly to ensure that each worshipper had the proper, flawless animal to offer to Jehovah. That practice, too, had become tainted by materialism and deception. The Mosaic law states that only the best of the flocks were to be offered (see Exodus 12). The Levites in charge of examining the worthiness of the offerings would often reject the sacrifice. The animal would then have to be exchanged for one that was deemed suitable. This was nothing more than a scam. The vendor would take the supposedly tainted animal—one that just moments before had likely been rejected as flawed—and, again for a fee, tout it as having passed inspection.

In the days leading up to the Passover, many merchants had set up shops outside Jerusalem on the roads leading into the city. Once the majority of the pilgrims had arrived, the hawkers moved into the temple court to ply their trade. Among the sellers were those who supplied pigeons to the poor, the lowliest of all sacrifices allowed by the law. The problem was that the price for a common bird was so exorbitant, the poor could not afford it as an offering, leaving them empty-handed.

Into the center of this maelstrom of greed taking place in His Father's house walked the Son of God, filled with righteous indignation. Such zeal had brought Him, early in His ministry, on a collision course with evil and those who practiced it. Not having learned the lesson Jesus had taught early in His ministry (see John 2), the money changers and vendors returned to the temple during the Passover celebration.

Author and teacher Charles Swindoll wrote of Jesus' response:

> Very often, people portray Jesus as the meek and mild teacher who taught His followers to love others as themselves, to avoid retaliation by turning the other cheek, to pursue peace, and to avoid judging others. While Jesus did indeed possess these qualities and teach these values, the picture is incomplete. These passages reveal that Jesus was more than the pale, languid figure often portrayed in art, on television, and in movies.[40]

John (2:17) concludes his record of this event with, "Then His disciples remembered that it was written, 'Zeal for Your house has eaten Me up.'" (See Psalm 69:9) The fervor of Jesus for His Father's house was not anger based; His response was not fueled by rage or resentment. No, His zeal was a holy protectiveness, a heavenly love for the earthly sign of God's presence, the symbol of His purpose, and a place of unhindered prayer. It was there that the Israelites, His people, were to go to pray and to worship Jehovah. It was there they were to hear the words of the patriarchs, poets, and prophets read. Sacrifice offered there was a prophetic picture of Messiah, the One standing in the Court of the Gentiles on that fateful day. Jesus did not respond in rage or foolhardiness, but with righteous indignation.

Why might this have been such a point of contention for Jesus? Pastor Eric Lenhart of North Main Street Church of God in Butler, Pennsylvania, proffered this explanation:

> The court of the Gentiles was the outer most court in the area of the Temple where only the gentiles, the handicapped, and the unclean could come to pray and worship. With all the activity of a common-day market place, there was no way that worship and prayer could be offered in such a place as this. With sheep bleating, coins jingling, doves cooing, and people sputtering deals to acquire a sacrifice from the merchants, the worshipers were inevitably crowded out. . . .

Jesus gave to those who would have otherwise been left by the wayside by those going into the inner courts to worship and pray; those more privileged to come closer to the Holy of Holies than they. And this is the true nature and character of God: always giving, always loving, always extending a hand of grace and forgiveness to those who honestly seek him.

The religious leaders and teachers of the law had forgotten God's true character. They had become so wrapped up in the legalities of the law, so puffed up by the pursuit of power and position, that they worshiped the structure of everyday life rather than the Giver of true life.[41]

## CARE FOR THE NEEDY

Matthew 21:14 (NKJV) tells us, "Then the blind and the lame came to Him in the temple, and He healed them." The remainder of Jesus' day was spent in ministry in the temple court. His righteous anger at the commercialization of His Father's house did not dissuade the sick and needy from reaching out to Him. Jesus didn't walk away after cleansing the temple; He met the needs of the individuals who were confined to worship in the court of the Gentiles. It was as close as they could get to the temple, and they were prohibited from access to the sacrificial altar. But on that particular day, the Promised One entered the court—and He healed them. Even with the horrors that would soon come upon Him, Jesus had great compassion for the lame and the blind who had remained in the temple. He reached out in love and took time to meet their needs.

The scribes and Pharisees were incensed both by the actions of Jesus and the joyous shouts of the children who followed Him.

Danish sculptor Bertel Thorvaldsen is said to have set about creating a statue of Jesus:

> He wished to see if the statue would cause the right reaction of heart in those who saw it. He brought a little child and bade him look at the statue, and asked him: "Who do you think that is?" The child looked, and then answered: "It is a great man." And Thorvaldsen knew that he had failed. So he scrapped his first statue and began again...when he had

finished, he brought the little child...and again asked the same question: "Who do you think that is?" And the child smiled and answered: "that is Jesus who said: 'Let the children come to me.'" And Thorvaldsen knew that this time he had succeeded. He submitted the statue to the test of the eyes of a child. When all is said and done that is no bad test .... The goodness which can meet the clear gaze of a child, and which can stand the test of a child's simplicity, is goodness indeed.[42]

The chief priests and scribes then turned their attention to the children. In my mind's eye I can see them skipping after Jesus as He made His way across the courtyard ministering to the sick and the lame. Matthew writes that the children were "crying out in the temple and saying, 'Hosanna to the Son of David!'" [The leaders approached Jesus and asked,] "Do You hear what these are saying?" And Jesus said to them, "Yes. Have you never read, 'Out of the mouth of babes and nursing infants You have perfected praise'?" (See Matthew 21:15–16 NKJV; Psalm 8:2.)

The holier-than-thou Pharisees took umbrage at the words of the children. How dare they praise this upstart from Nazareth? As if Jesus were deaf, they demanded to know if He had heard the shouts. The children's ready acceptance of the Man and His miracles was spontaneous. Jesus responded to the criticism by quoting the words of the psalmist. Just three chapters before this discourse, in Matthew 18:3–4, Jesus had told the crowd gathered around Him, "Assuredly, I say to you, unless you are converted and become as little children, you will by no means enter the kingdom of heaven" (NKJV).

Rather than repent of their greed, the murderous desires enthroned in the hearts of the leaders roiled to the surface. How dare this Jesus try to discredit them? The conspirators then left the temple to mobilize their allies, rouse the rabble, set the trap that would ensnare Jesus of Nazareth, and end His influence once and for all.

> Then He [Jesus] left them and went out
> of the city to Bethany, and He lodged there.
> Matthew 21:17 NKJV

# CHAPTER 12

*For I tell you, unless your righteousness
exceeds that of the scribes and Pharisees, you
will never enter the kingdom of heaven.*

MATTHEW 5:20 ESV

Tuesday of Passion Week brought Jesus face-to-face
yet again with the scribes and Pharisees. These men,
who seemed to constantly plot the end of the earthly ministry of Jesus, are mentioned some sixty times in Matthew,
Mark, and Luke but only once in John as the disciple retells
the story of the woman taken in adultery. It was the duty
of the scribes, scholarly men, to study the law of Moses,
reproduce it, and pen interpretations of it. They were very
serious and exacting as they went about their duties. It was
those men who so correctly preserved the Old Testament for

posterity. Scribes belonged predominantly to the sect of the Pharisees and were held in high regard by the people. This despite the man-made traditions that were added to the law, burdens that made it almost impossible for anyone to fulfill God's Word.

The account in Matthew 21:18–19 of Jesus having cursed the fig tree is filled with symbolism. The unproductive tree represented the dead religion of the Pharisees—one based solely on works with no allowance for grace or hope. It offered no sustenance; it was a dead, lifeless tree with no fruit planted in dry ground. While the scribes and Pharisees looked down their collective, hypocritical noses at anyone who transgressed the law, Jesus reached out in love and mercy. Matthew relates very simply that Jesus was physically hungry and looking for a snack. He made for the nearest wayside fig tree. It looked the part of a healthy fig tree with branches and leaves but was devoid of a single piece of fruit. It was useless, and so was cursed. It was an amazing sight and a divine illustration that "profession without practice is condemned."[43]

> And when the disciples saw it, they marveled, saying, "How did the fig tree wither away so soon?" Matthew 21:20 NKJV

## TUESDAY IN THE TEMPLE

When Jesus and His followers arrived at the temple the following morning, the Pharisees were apparently still stinging from their encounter with deity the day before:

> Now when He came into the temple, the chief priests and the elders of the people confronted Him as He was teaching, and said, "By what authority are You doing these things? And who gave You this authority?"
> Matthew 21:23 NKJV

Instead of asking, as did the jailer in Acts 16, "What must I do to be saved?" the Pharisees questioned Jesus regarding from whom He had obtained the authority to teach, preach, and heal. It revealed yet again that the quest for power and authority outpaced the desire for righteousness and holiness.

In Matthew 23:13 (NKJV), Jesus delivers the first "woe" to the scribes and Pharisees:

> But woe to you, scribes and Pharisees, hypocrites! For you shut up the kingdom of heaven against men; for you neither go in yourselves, nor do you allow those who are entering to go in.

William Barclay, the great Scots Bible expositor, wrote of that particular group:

> To Jesus the Scribes and Pharisees were men who were acting a part. What He meant was this. Their whole idea of religion consisted in outward observance, the wearing of elaborate phylacteries and tassels, the meticulous observance of the rules and regulations of the Law. But in their hearts there was bitterness and envy and price and arrogance. To Jesus these Scribes and Pharisees were men who, under a mask of elaborate godliness, concealed hearts in which the most godless feelings and emotions held sway . . . . Jesus' condemnation of these Scribes and Pharisees is that they have not themselves entered the Kingdom, and they have shut the door in the faces of those who are seeking entry to the Kingdom . . . . The Pharisees believed that to do God's will was to observe their thousands of petty rules and regulations.[44]

Outwardly, the men appeared to be precise and faithful keepers of the law, but Jesus took them to task severely in the entire chapter of Matthew 23 with warning after warning and woe upon woe. In verses 27–28 (NKJV), Jesus counsels them with:

> "Woe to you, scribes and Pharisees, hypocrites! For you are like whitewashed tombs which indeed appear beautiful outwardly, but inside are full of dead men's bones and all uncleanness. Even so you also outwardly appear righteous to men, but inside you are full of hypocrisy and lawlessness.

Dr. John F. Walvoord, long-time president of Dallas Theological Seminary, wrote of this condemnation:

> Only Matthew records this scathing denunciation of these religious leaders of the Jews. These woes, in contrast to the Beatitudes, denounce false religion as utterly abhorrent to God and worthy of severe condemnation. No passage in the Bible is more biting, more pointed, or more severe than this pronouncement of Christ upon the Pharisees. It is significant that He singled them out, as opposed to the Sadducees, who were more

liberal, and the Herodians, who were the politicians. The Pharisees, while attempting to honor the Word of God and manifesting an extreme form of religious observance, were actually the farthest from God.[45]

## THE PRAISE OF GOD
## OR THE PRAISE OF MEN

The scribes should have realized as they studied that God alone is to be the recipient of the praise of men, but in fact, the majority of the recorders were enamored by the adulation *they* received from the people. Wearing his white linen robe, with an identical mantel fringed on the bottom, the scribe would parade his occupation, and thus his knowledge, through the streets of Jerusalem. Surrounded by those clad in homespun garments, the scholarly man would clearly stand out among the throngs who daily trod the highways and byways of the city.

As the scribe made his way around the city, men would rise when he walked by as a sign of respect for his office, and referred to him as rabbi and master. A scribe commanded the highest place of honor at a banquet and enjoyed a reserved seat in the local synagogue.

In Luke 20, Jesus was teaching in the temple when challenged by the chief priests and scribes; He responded with parables. As He neared the end of His discourse, Luke 21:1–4 (NKJV) gives us this picture:

> And He looked up and saw the rich putting their gifts into the treasury, and He saw also a certain poor widow putting in two mites. So He said, "Truly I say to you that this poor widow has put in more than all; for all these out of their abundance have put in offerings for God, but she out of her poverty put in all the livelihood that she had."

In Luke 21, Jesus tried to get the scribes and Pharisees to focus on what was important as He pointed out the poor widow making her way to one of the trumpet-shaped containers that stood along a wall in the Court of the Women. Made of metal rather than stone, the cylinders were receptacles for offerings—ones that would resound with the noise of coins being dropped inside. As all eyes turned toward the humble woman making her way toward the offering container, it was apparent from the sound of it that she had dropped only two tiny copper coins (lepton) inside. Together they were worth about one-eighth of a cent in US currency. *Forum Ancient Coins* has this to say about the offering:

> The lepton is the very smallest denomination and is probably the true "widow's mite." In fact, the lepton is probably the lowest denomination coin ever struck by any nation in all of history! Lepton and prutah were carelessly and crudely struck, usually off center . . . . Because they circulated for a long period, they are usually very worn. Legends are almost always unreadable. The actual size of a prutah is less than 1/2 inch in diameter. A lepton is usually about the same diameter as a pencil eraser.[46]

Were the scribes and Pharisees impressed? Unlikely! But Jesus was blessed by her offering. Not only did she offer all the coins she possessed, she offered her next purchase of food, raising the possibility that she might not meet her own survival needs. The scribes thought all they needed was for someone to take care of them—to provide food, clothing, shelter—and they labored diligently to add to their list of patrons. The poor widow was the perfect example of generosity, faith, and commitment.

For their work in the temple, the scribes lived on contributions and subsidies, and were not paid a salary. Often scribes were supported by a specific family that was held in high regard for underwriting the scholarly copyist. Because families sometimes placed their wealth at the disposal of one of the scribes, there was ample room for abuse associated with the practice. Although those men were to use the Word to point men to Jehovah, all too often they pointed only to themselves and their wants and needs. The scribes totally missed the golden opportunity to become spiritually rich and were instead poor in the grace and favor of God.

## "NOT WILLING THAT ANY SHOULD PERISH"[47]

Although Jesus would have but one day of rest and reflection before facing the cross, He spent Tuesday reaching out to those who would ultimately betray Him. In parable after parable, encounter after encounter, Jesus was challenged by the Pharisees on the practice of paying taxes (see Matthew 22:15–21), the Sadducees on the resurrection (vv. 23–33), and the scribes on the subject of which commandment is greatest (vv. 34–40). At the end of the day, Jesus confronts the Pharisees with the question:

"What do you think about the Christ? Whose Son is He?" They said to Him, "The Son of David." He said to them, "How then does David in the Spirit call Him 'Lord,' saying: 'The Lord said to my Lord, "Sit at My right hand, till I make Your enemies Your footstool"'? If David then calls Him 'Lord,' how is He his Son?" And no one was able to answer Him a word, nor from that day on did anyone dare question Him anymore. Matthew 22:42–46 NKJV

Sadly, the majority of the religionists of Jesus' day missed the opportunity to embrace Him and His message. English poet Dante Gabriel Rossetti wrote: "Look in my face; my name is Might-have-been; I am also call'd No-more, Too-late, Farewell."[48]

Tuesday of Passion Week ended with Jesus and His disciples walking to the Mount of Olives on the east side of Jerusalem. As they were leaving the city, some of the disciples who perhaps had not visited Jerusalem often—or had never been in the Holy City—turned to view its walls. According to Barclay, this is what they would have seen:

...marble plated with gold, and it shone and glinted in the sun so that a man could scarcely bear to look at it . . . . The Temple area was surrounded by great porches...upheld by pillars cut out of solid blocks of marble in one piece . . . . At the corners of the Temple angle stones have been found which measure from 20 to 40 feet in length, and which weigh more than 100 tons . . . . Little wonder that the Galilaean fishermen looked with awe on these vast stones, and these amazing buildings, and called Jesus' attention to them.[49]

## A LONGING LOOK AT THE TEMPLE MOUNT

The disciples were awed by the sight of the temple glimmering in the afternoon sun, but Jesus saw a different sight as He turned to look:

And Jesus said to them, "Do you not see all these things? Assuredly, I say to you, not one stone shall be left here upon another, that shall not be thrown down." Matthew 24:2 NKJV

Instead of reliving the day's events, the triumphal entry into the city, the people clamoring for Him to be declared King, Jesus remembered how He had wept over the city that lay before Him, wept over its inglorious future. In AD 70, Jesus' prophecy was fulfilled. The Romans, exasperated with repeated rebellions in Judea, marched into Jerusalem and demolished the temple—stone by stone. Is there any wonder Jesus cried? William Barclay penned a truth that would be well to remember today:

> Jesus knew that the way of power politics can only end in doom. The man and the nation which will not take the way of God are heading for disaster.[50]

The whole of Matthew 24 has come to be known as the "Olivet Discourse." In that chapter, as well as Mark 13 and Luke 21, Jesus gave the disciples an overview of what the future held, first for Jerusalem, and second at the end of the age. Fuller Theological Seminary professor George Eldon Ladd wrote:

> There can be little doubt but that the disciples thought of the destruction of the temple as one of the events accompanying the end of the age and the coming of the eschatological Kingdom of God.[51]

Jesus had spent the days before teaching His followers

through parables; now He was to deliver His most important discourse. Instead of giving a rousing "Crown Me King" speech, He spared nothing with His warning of what was to come to their beloved city:

> For days will come upon you when your enemies will build an embankment around you, surround you and close you in on every side, and level you, and your children within you, to the ground; and they will not leave in you one stone upon another, because you did not know the time of your visitation.
> Luke 19:43–44 NKJV

One of Satan's most effective tools is the word *tomorrow*. It was Thomas Jefferson who said, "Never put off until tomorrow what you can do today." How much more important that is when dealing with the soul's salvation. No man knows the day or the hour when Jesus will return and set His feet once again on the Temple Mount. On this day, He was preparing to lay down His life so that those who would believe on Him in the ages to come will have no fear of tomorrow. We have the promise that "whoever believes in Him should not perish but have everlasting life" (John 3:16 NKJV).

# CHAPTER 13

Wednesday would likely have been a day of rest and preparation for Jesus, as there is no mention in the Gospels of any activities surrounding Him on that day. It was, however, a pivotal day for Judas, the betrayer, one numbered among the twelve disciples. Throughout the New Testament and beyond, that is how he has been known—the Betrayer of Jesus.

Only God knows how long he may have been fantasizing about forcing Jesus to declare His kingship, if that was, indeed, Judas Iscariot's excuse. How had Satan tempted this disciple into treachery? Did Judas believe that if Christ was crowned King of Judah, the disciples would have elevated roles in His kingdom? Was the betrayer driven by egomania? Or was it just simple avarice that prompted Judas? If so, perhaps the singular best example can be found in 1 Timothy 6:10 (KJV): "For the love of money is the root of all evil: which while some coveted after, they have erred from the faith, and pierced themselves through with many sorrows."

Jesus knew from the very beginning which of His trusted companions would be the one to betray Him. With that insight, why did Jesus entrust this particular disciple with the money bag? Why did He not just leave Judas behind and take another more trustworthy disciple? Could it have had to do with a parable Jesus told His followers—the one in Matthew 13? The enemy had crept into the wheat field and surreptitiously scattered tares in with the wheat. Tares as they began to grow looked very much like the young shoots of wheat that burst forth from the ground. It was almost impossible to distinguish one from the other. The farmer was asked if the tares should be pulled up, and declined:

No...you'll uproot the wheat if you do. Let
both grow together until the harvest. Then
I will tell the harvesters to sort out the

weeds, tie them into bundles, and burn them, and to put the wheat in the barn. Matthew 13:29–30 NLT

Perhaps Jesus was thinking of how many of His disciples would be deeply wounded by Judas' treachery, and would turn back in disappointment. They were likely not aware of the disciple's past history. In John 12:1–6 (NIV), after Jesus had set His face toward Jerusalem, we see a picture of Judas and his deceit:

Six days before the Passover, Jesus came to Bethany, where Lazarus lived, whom Jesus had raised from the dead. Here a dinner was given in Jesus' honor. Martha served, while Lazarus was among those reclining at the table with him. Then Mary [Martha's sister] took about a pint of pure nard, an expensive perfume; she poured it on Jesus' feet and wiped his feet with her hair. And the house was filled with the fragrance of the perfume. But one of his disciples, Judas Iscariot, who was later to betray him, objected, "Why wasn't this perfume sold and the money given to the poor? It was worth a year's wages." He did not say this because he cared about the poor but because he was a thief; as keeper of the money bag, he used to help himself to what was put into it.

## THE BETRAYER BETRAYS

After all the teaching, all the miracles, all the prayers, all the fellowship, still Judas was willing to hand Jesus over to the authorities. An article from the campus of Columbia International University in Columbia, South Carolina, raised an interesting question:

Why did Satan select Judas as his agent, his "mole" within the band of disciples? What would suggest to Satan that, rather than the four fishermen or naive Nathanael, this man could be tempted with position and power? One answer may lie in Judas' origin. His name, Judas Iscarioth, (Ish, "man of" Kerioth) identifies him as a citizen of Kerioth, a small village about twenty miles south of Hebron. The region had been settled by Edomites, as reflected in its Latin name, Idumea. Idumeans were in the audience for

Jesus' Sermon on the Mount (Mark 3:7-8). The night before that event, He had selected the Twelve, including Judas (Luke 6:12-16). Jesus' other disciples were Galileans, but Judas was apparently an Idumean, a descendant of Esau. Jesus and His other disciples traced their ancestry back to Jacob, but if Judas were an Idumean, he would have been a descendant of Esau, Jacob's alienated brother. Judas' probable connection with "the other line" of Isaac's sons may not have been a factor in Satan's recruitment of this special agent . . . but, then, it would certainly have had historical precedent![52]

On that particular Wednesday, Judas stealthily made his way to the high priest and members of the Sanhedrin, the supreme council of religious leaders. Among the men were Sadducees, Pharisees, and scribes, all jealous of Jesus' power, His popularity, and the praises heaped upon Him. Jesus' message was one of grace and compassion; theirs one of works, works, and more works!

There were doctrines on which the various sects agreed and tenets on which they disagreed. Some were liberal, some were legalistic, but they all seemed to agree on one thing: Jesus of Nazareth had to go! Nothing short of death would satisfy their animosity. For three long days, He had wreaked havoc in their domain—routing the moneychangers, healing the lame and diseased, ministering to the people through parables, and foiling the tricks and plots of the rulers. They were incensed and determined that it must stop. Surely they questioned who might be the one to come alongside them and provide a way out of their predicament. It wasn't long before "Satan entered into Judas called Iscariot, who was of the number of the twelve" (Luke 22:3 ESV). No one had to coerce Judas; no persuasion was needed. He walked into the courtroom and bartered with them for the life of Jesus.

Almost from the time He burst on the scene, the Jewish authorities had tried to trap Jesus, and now He was being handed over to them on a platter lined with thirty pieces of silver—the legal price of a slave. In Zechariah 11:12–13 (NKJV) we read:

> Then I said to them, "If it is agreeable to you, give me my wages; and if not, refrain." So they weighed out for my wages thirty pieces of silver. And the Lord said to me, "Throw it to the potter"—that princely price they set

on me. So I took the thirty pieces of silver and threw them into the house of the Lord for the potter.

Judas would never know what might have been had he remained faithful to Jesus, the Messiah. Rather, he would eventually have to face the consequences of his choices. And make a proactive choice, he did: he chose death rather than life! It was a moment in time that would echo throughout eternity. It was fulfillment of the prophecy pronounced by Caiaphas in John 11:47–52 (ESV):

> So the chief priests and the Pharisees gathered the council and said, "What are we to do? For this man performs many signs. If we let him go on like this, everyone will believe in him, and the Romans will come and take away both our place and our nation." But one of them, Caiaphas, who was high priest that year, said to them, "You know nothing at all. Nor do you understand that it is better for you that one man should die for the people, not that the whole nation should perish." He did not say this of his own accord, but being high priest that year he prophesied that

Jesus would die for the nation, and not for the nation only, but also to gather into one the children of God who are scattered abroad.

It was the duty of the high priest to select the lamb that would be slain during the Passover. Caiaphas, with his machinations against Jesus, had no understanding that he had just chosen Jesus to die for the sins of not just the Jewish people but "the children of God who are scattered abroad."

Unknowingly, Judas had become a pawn in the hands of those who wished to be rid of Jesus. But soon the weight of his actions would come crashing down on him as Wednesday morphed into Thursday and the observance of the Passover meal began to take precedence. Did shame keep Judas away from the observance? Not at all! His conscience seared, he took his seat at the table with Jesus and the other eleven disciples. Unlike Jesus, who would not be tempted by Satan during His forty-day desert sojourn, Judas paid heed to the Enemy of his soul.

## BETRAYED BY A BROTHER

Joseph in the Old Testament was a type of Christ. Satan tried to end his life through the betrayal of his brothers. When Joseph was finally given the opportunity to retaliate, he instead offered grace. In Genesis 50:20 (NLT), we read his merciful response when his brothers stood before him:

> You intended to harm me, but God intended
> it all for good. He brought me to this position
> so I could save the lives of many people.

Max Lucado, renowned author and pastor of Oak Hills Church in San Antonio, Texas, wrote of Satan's plan for Joseph, a scenario that could well be applied to Judas' plan against Jesus:

> In God's hands intended evil becomes
> eventual good. Joseph tied himself to the
> pillar of this promise and held on for dear life.
> Nothing in his story glosses over the pres-
> ence of evil. Quite the contrary. Bloodstains,
> tearstains are everywhere. Joseph's heart was
> rubbed raw against the rocks of disloyalty
> and miscarried justice. Yet time and time
> again God redeemed the pain. The torn robe
> became a royal one. The pit became a palace.
> The broken family grew old together. The
> very acts intended to destroy God's servant
> turned out to strengthen him.

"You meant evil against me," Joseph told his brothers, using a Hebrew verb that traces its meaning to "weave" or "plait."

"You wove evil," he was saying, "but God rewove it together for good."

God, the Master Weaver. He stretches the yarn and intertwines the colors, the ragged twine with the velvet strings, the pains with the pleasures. Nothing escapes His reach. Every king, despot, weather pattern, and molecule are at His command. He passes the shuttle back and forth across the generations, and as He does, a design emerges.[53]

It seems that Judas, the betrayer, had for some time been planning how he might betray Jesus. He knew when and how he would make his approach and what he would do when the time came. Ultimately, as with Joseph, God would use Judas' betrayal to weave a garment of good.

But when the sun rose the morning after he had met with the Sanhedrin, Judas, keeper of the purse, hurried out to help with preparations for Passover.

# CHAPTER 14

*The next day John saw Jesus coming toward*
*him, and said, "Behold! The Lamb of God*
*who takes away the sin of the world!*

JOHN 1:29 NKJV

When Jesus and the disciples arose on the morning
of Passover, our Lord gave specific instructions
for the day's events:

On the first of the Days of Unleavened
Bread, the disciples came to Jesus and said,
"Where do you want us to prepare your Pass-
over meal?"

He said, "Enter the city. Go up to a certain
man and say, 'The Teacher says, My time is
near. I and my disciples plan to celebrate the
Passover meal at your house.'" The disciples

followed Jesus' instructions to the letter, and prepared the Passover meal. Matthew 26:17–19 MSG

Celebrating Passover was scripted, down to the rule stating that the Holy Day must be observed within the ramparts of Jerusalem. Just as Jesus had instructed, the men, Peter and John, walked inside the city walls and saw a man carrying a large water vessel. That would have been an unusual sight in ancient Israel; it was generally women's work to fill and transport the water vessels from the communal well. Such an occurrence would have caught the attention of the disciples.

The men fell into step behind the one bearing the pot and followed him home. There they explained their mission: Jesus wished to observe Passover in his home. The man, whom some surmise might have been John Mark[54], the author of the gospel of Mark, showed them an upper room where they might enjoy the feast.

The disciples set to work ridding the house of any leaven that might remain. They then went to the marketplace to find a lamb suitable for sacrifice in the temple. The lamb then had to be roasted and the unleavened bread baked. Wine had to be purchased and the accoutrements for the meal had to be prepared. It would have been a very busy day for them, and all had to be completed by sundown.

## THE SYMBOLISM OF PASSOVER

It must have been a bittersweet night for Jesus. He knew what awaited in the hours ahead—the humiliation, the excruciating pain, the suffering. Yet "for the joy that was set before Him endured the cross, despising the shame, and has sat down at the right hand of the throne of God (Hebrews 12:2 NKJV)," Jesus would complete the work He was sent to accomplish. On that long-ago night in Jerusalem, the Passover observance was to be a picture of deliverance and salvation available only through the Messiah. The prophet Isaiah provided a clear embodiment of what many have called the Suffering Savior (Isaiah 53:3–7 NIV):

> He was despised and rejected by mankind,
> a man of suffering, and familiar with pain.
> Like one from whom people hide their faces
> he was despised, and we held him in low
> esteem. Surely he took up our pain and bore
> our suffering, yet we considered him pun-
> ished by God, stricken by him, and afflicted.
> But he was pierced for our transgressions,

he was crushed for our iniquities; the punishment that brought us peace was on him, and by his wounds we are healed. We all, like sheep, have gone astray, each of us has turned to our own way; and the Lord has laid on him the iniquity of us all. He was oppressed and afflicted, yet he did not open his mouth; he was led like a lamb to the slaughter, and as a sheep before its shearers is silent, so he did not open his mouth.

Pastor Randy Moll of Good Shepherd Lutheran Church in Rogers, Arkansas, wrote of this passage in Isaiah:

His form and appearance was nothing unusual so as to draw people to Him or permit them to recognize Him as the Messiah. And, as Jesus carried out His ministry, calling upon all to repent and believe the good news of forgiveness and life in Him, He was despised and rejected.

The religious leaders of Israel hated Him and viewed Him as a threat to their system of worship and sacrifice. The religiously conservative Pharisees hated Him because He pointed out their inner transgressions and failures to keep God's law by loving Him first and foremost and then also loving their neighbor as themselves. The liberal Sadducees hated Him, for He pointed out their unbelief and rejection of the teaching of the Holy Scriptures. Many of the common people recognized His great power and longed to see His miracles; but still, for the most part, they failed to recognize Him as the holy Son of God come into this world a true man to save sinners.[55]

## THE PURPOSE OF PASSOVER

Passover, as well as the other feasts celebrated by the Israelites, was conducted to bring the people together as a nation and to remind them of Jehovah's deliverance from bondage. The observances were spiritual in that they presented a picture of the truth of iniquity and immorality, the verdict that accompanied the breaking of God's laws, the pardon provided by a blood sacrifice, and the inherent need to praise God for His grace and mercy.

The sun rose steadily in the eastern sky on the morning

of the Passover celebration. A lamb had been selected—a male without spot or defect of any kind (see Exodus 12:5). The high priest was surely unaware that he had chosen the Lamb when bartering with Judas for the price of his disloyalty. When baptized by John in the river Jordan, Jesus had been referred to as the Lamb of God (see John 1:29). Born to be the Passover Lamb, Jesus was now fulfilling those requirements: He was a male with no birth defects and had been in Jerusalem for four days prior to Passover. The very fact that He was without sin qualified Jesus to be the Lamb of God—a human lamb who would shoulder the sins of all mankind.

Some of the disciples had questioned Jesus about where the observance of Passover would take place. In Matthew 26:17–19 (NIV) we read:

> On the first day of the Festival of Unleavened Bread, the disciples came to Jesus and asked, "Where do you want us to make preparations for you to eat the Passover?" He replied, "Go into the city to a certain man and tell him, 'The Teacher says: My appointed time is near. I am going to celebrate the Passover with my disciples at your house.'" So the

disciples did as Jesus had directed them and prepared the Passover.

The life of Jesus had been offered for the price of a lamb. So Judas, who had agreed to betray Jesus, took the sum offered by the Jewish authorities, pocketed it, and went on his way to partake of the Passover Seder with Jesus and his fellow disciples who had gathered to commemorate Passover before Jesus' death. Although there is no scriptural basis for the terminology, the event is referred to by New Testament Believers as the Lord's Supper, the Last Supper, or simply Communion.

## THE ELEMENTS OF PASSOVER

A Passover lamb would have been chosen to be roasted and eaten as the traditional four-course meal celebrated by Jesus and His disciples. Unlike today's often too-quickly observed Lord's Supper, the Seder could take several hours. The table would likely have been set with at least four cups, the meaning of which we find in Exodus 6:6–7:

- ✧ The Cup of Blessing—"I am the Lord."

- ✧ The Cup of Judgment—"I will bring you out from under the yoke."

✧ The Cup of Redemption—"I will redeem
  you with an outstretched arm."

✧ The Cup of Praise—"I will take you as my
  own people, and I will be your God."

Biblical scholars are unsure if each disciple had
four cups at his place setting, or if those were allotted
only to Jesus. We do know that at least the third cup—
the Cup of Redemption—was shared with all at the
table.

It was, however, after the first cup that Jesus removed
His robe and took on the role of servant to wash the feet
of His disciples. This was a role that generally fell to the
individual of the lowest rank at the table. If that were Peter,
it might explain his horror that Jesus was about to bow and
wash his feet. It had been in Capernaum as recorded in Mark
9:35, that Jesus said, "Anyone who wants to be first must be
the very last, and the servant of all" (NIV).

With the Cup of Judgment, the bitter herbs (maror) were
served—a representation of the terrible bitterness of sin.
Perhaps it is at this juncture that Jesus revealed His betrayal
and betrayer. As Jesus distributed the bread and wine, He
was informing His disciples that He was the Passover Lamb
for whom they had been waiting. In 1 Corinthians 5:7, Paul

referred to Christ as "our Passover lamb." And just as none of the bones of the Passover lamb were to be broken, so none of Jesus' bones were broken as He was beaten, scourged, and hung on the cross.

And here we find one of the saddest exchanges in the Gospels—one of Love reaching out to save. *The Message* gives us a very contemporary yet graphic translation of the exchange between Jesus and Judas:

> After sunset, he and the Twelve were sitting around the table. During the meal, he said, "I have something hard but important to say to you: One of you is going to hand me over to the conspirators." They were stunned, and then began to ask, one after another, "It isn't me, is it, Master?" Jesus answered, "The one who hands me over is someone I eat with daily, one who passes me food at the table. In one sense the Son of Man is entering into a way of treachery well-marked by the Scriptures—no surprises here. In another sense that man who turns him in, turns traitor to the Son of Man—better never to have been born than do this!" Then Judas,

already turned traitor, said, "It isn't me, is it, Rabbi?" Jesus said, "Don't play games with me, Judas." Matthew 26:20–25

Perhaps this was a last warning, a final plea to the man whom Jesus knew would betray Him. Could he have been saying to Judas, "Please think about what you are planning to do. It's not too late. Return the silver and repent"? Knowing that Judas possessed an unrepentant heart, "Jesus said to him, 'What you are going to do, do quickly'" (John 13:27b ESV).

The next cup was to be the Cup of Redemption. A talented blogger with "Fishing from the Abyss," wrote of Judas' departure:

> Notice that, since Judas leaves immediately after eating the bitter herbs (the only item dipped from a dish as part of the meal), he does not share in the Cup of Redemption, and he is left with the symbolic taste of sin in his mouth, which is never washed away before his death, the following day.[56]

The Cup of Redemption is the same cup shared by Believers. Jesus said, "This do in remembrance of me" (Luke

22:19 KJV). Observance of the Lord's Supper is symbolic of the relationship between Jesus and His followers; and it is also a promise of an event to come. Jesus said, "Truly I tell you, I will not drink again from the fruit of the vine until that day when I drink it new in the kingdom of God" (Mark 14:25 NIV).

Pastor and teacher Dr. John MacArthur wrote:

> As He sat in that secluded room with His disciples, Christ knew what was going to happen. He was preparing Himself and His closest friends for the moment He would be handed over for execution. Over the centuries millions of Passover lambs had been slaughtered—each of them foreshadowing the sacrifice Jesus was about to make to free God's people from the bondage of their sins. The symbols and shadows of the Passover were about to cease—the true Lamb had arrived. And at exactly the hour of slaughter on Friday afternoon, He would die, the veil in the temple would be ripped from top to bottom, and the system of sacrifice would come to an end.[57]

They may have sung the first part of the Hallel, but scripture does not reveal that. Christ chose the breaking of the matzah and dipping it in the bitter herbs to indicate that Judas would be the one to betray Him. What sorrow of soul our Lord must have felt, knowing that one who had walked with Him for three years was about to hand Him over to be crucified. Throughout that meal, Jesus was preparing His closest friends for the moment He would be executed.

With the third matzah Jesus instituted what we now call the Lord's Supper. He broke the bread saying, "This is my body given for you; do this in remembrance of me." (Luke 22:19) He then took the third cup of wine, blessed it and said, "This is the cup of the new covenant in my blood; do this, whenever you drink it, in remembrance of me." (1 Corinthians 11:25) Matthew then recorded in chapter 26, verse 30 that the group sang a hymn—likely the second part of the Hallel and then departed for the Mount of Olives.

Over the centuries millions of Passover lambs had been slaughtered—each of them foreshadowing the sacrifice Jesus was about to make to free God's people from the bondage of their sins. The symbols and shadows of the Passover were about to be brought to light—the true Lamb had arrived. And at exactly the hour of slaughter on Friday afternoon, He would die, the veil in the temple would be ripped from top to bottom, and the system of sacrifice would come to an end. It was in those final moments with His disciples that Christ transformed the elements of the Passover celebration, creating a new memorial to God's gracious deliverance of His people.

# CHAPTER 15

*And when they had sung a hymn, they*
*went out to the Mount of Olives.*

MATTHEW 26:30 NKJV

After partaking of the Cup of Praise and singing the *hallel* (Psalm 113–118), Jesus and His disciples—minus Judas, of course—went out to the Mount of Olives and into the garden of Gethsemane. The requirement to stay within the walls of Jerusalem until after midnight—the hour the death angel visited Egypt—had been fulfilled, and it was now permissible to leave the upper room. As they made their way from the city, the little band would have had to cross a rivulet known as Kidron. For much of the year, the brook was but a trickle, but at Passover the blood of the sacrifices was channeled from the Temple Mount into the stream, now overflowing with it. I wonder: Did Jesus compare that to the stream that would soon flow from His hands, feet, and side? Poet William Cowper wrote:

> There is a fountain filled with blood
>
> drawn from Emmanuel's veins;
>
> And sinners plunged beneath that
>
> flood lose all their guilty stains.
>
> Lose all their guilty stains, lose
>
> all their guilty stains;
>
> And sinners plunged beneath that flood
>
> lose all their guilty stains . . . .
>
> Dear dying Lamb, Thy precious
>
> blood shall never lose its power
>
> Till all the ransomed church of
>
> God be saved, to sin no more.
>
> Be saved, to sin no more, be
>
> saved, to sin no more;
>
> Till all the ransomed church of God
>
> be saved, to sin no more.[58]

Jesus and His followers entered the garden. Mark described the scene in 14:32–36 (NKJV):

> Then they came to a place which was
>
> named Gethsemane; and He said to His

disciples, "Sit here while I pray." And He took Peter, James, and John with Him, and He began to be troubled and deeply distressed. Then He said to them, "My soul is exceedingly sorrowful, even to death. Stay here and watch." He went a little farther, and fell on the ground, and prayed that if it were possible, the hour might pass from Him. And He said, "Abba, Father, all things are possible for You. Take this cup away from Me; nevertheless, not what I will, but what You will."

Gethsemane is translated as "oil press." John MacArthur says of the garden:

It probably belonged to a friend of the Lord. While it is famous in our day, and still exists just outside the city of Jerusalem, in the Lord's day it was probably a small garden enclosed by a wall and guarded by a gate . . . . It was a place Jesus often visited with His men, Luke 22:39. Gethsemane seems to have been a refuge for the Lord. It was a place where He could find solitude from the crowds and ministry that occupied His life. It was a place where He could go to find a private moment to commune with His Father. It was a sanctuary from the attacks of His enemies. It was a place of refreshment from the long days of ministry. It was a special place for the Lord and His men. The name *Gethsemane* is Aramaic in origin...and [was] a place where olive trees grew and produced their fruit. The olives were collected, placed in a press and the precious olive oil was extracted from the olives under intense pressure . . . . On this night, our Lord would enter the *"Olive Press"* and the sweet oil of grace and submission to the Father would be extracted from the Lord's life. For Jesus, the garden of Gethsemane would be a place of intense pressures. Our text tells us about some of the pressures He faced that night.[59]

## THE PAIN OF GETHSEMANE

Perhaps it was there in the garden that Jesus really understood the severity of the task ahead of Him. He would have read the words of Isaiah the prophet in chapter 53, verses

4–10. Again, *The Message* gives these verses such a graphic quality:

> But the fact is, it was our pains he carried—
> our disfigurements, all the things wrong with
> us. We thought he brought it on himself, that
> God was punishing him for his own failures.
> But it was our sins that did that to him, that
> ripped and tore and crushed him—our sins!
> He took the punishment, and that made us
> whole. Through his bruises we get healed.
> We're all like sheep who've wandered off and
> gotten lost. We've all done our own thing,
> gone our own way. And God has piled all our
> sins, everything we've done wrong, on him,
> on him. He was beaten, he was tortured, but
> he didn't say a word. Like a lamb taken to be
> slaughtered and like a sheep being sheared,
> he took it all in silence. Justice miscarried,
> and he was led off—and did anyone really
> know what was happening? He died without
> a thought for his own welfare, beaten bloody
> for the sins of my people. They buried him
> with the wicked, threw him in a grave with

a rich man, even though he'd never hurt a soul or said one word that wasn't true. Still, it's what God had in mind all along, to crush him with pain. The plan was that he give himself as an offering for sin so that he'd see life come from it—life, life, and more life. And God's plan will deeply prosper through him.

There in the garden of Gethsemane, it all came flooding in—what He must endure, how He must die, the degradation and pain of crucifixion—and it was overwhelming. Luke paints the picture of Jesus' travail as He prayed the prayer that never fails:

And He was withdrawn from them about a stone's throw, and He knelt down and prayed, saying, "Father, if it is Your will, take this cup away from Me; *nevertheless not My will, but Yours, be done.*" Then an angel appeared to Him from heaven, strengthening Him. And being in agony, He prayed more earnestly. Then His sweat became like great drops of blood falling down to the ground. Luke 22:41–44 NKJV, emphasis mine

It is at this point, I believe, the knowledge that He was to be the sacrificial Lamb hit like the force of a huge boulder rolling downhill and slamming into the valley below. He, Jesus of Nazareth, was the "Lamb slain from the foundation of the world" (Revelation 13:8 KJV).

Perhaps it was then that His "sweat was as it were great drops of blood falling down to the ground" (Luke 22:44 KJV). Was it here that He began to feel the burden of the sins of all mankind descending on His sinless shoulders—lust, greed, anger, murder, debauchery, hatred? He who was about to be betrayed into the hands of His accusers was served a foretaste of what would happen the following day.

The Son of Man was so overcome by the magnitude of what He was about to face that He prayed in desperation. Jesus was staggered at the bitterness of the cup He had been asked to drink, at the cross He had been asked to shoulder, and yet He just as desperately wanted to do the Father's will. He desired that more than He valued His own life. Jesus was about to be crushed by the weight of sin just as the olives were crushed by the stone press. Pressed from our Savior was not oil, but rather a plan for our salvation fueled by a love that will not let us go.

## THE AGONY OF BETRAYAL

While Jesus was in a garden permeated with agony, Judas was in a room filled with jubilation. Jesus of Nazareth, the One who had foiled the Pharisees again and again, was about to be seized and sacrificed. Judas must have swelled with self-importance. He would be the one to force the hand of the Messiah; he would be the one to receive the accolades of the other disciples when they took their rightful places in the kingdom Judas thought was to come. He was ready to march with the troops that were to be dispatched to arrest Jesus:

> So Judas came to the garden, guiding a detachment of soldiers [KJV reads "band of men"] and some officials from the chief priests and the Pharisees. They were carrying torches, lanterns and weapons. John 18:3 NIV

Rising from the rocky ground, Jesus turned to His sleeping disciples and roused them. As they stretched and rubbed the sleep from their eyes, the sounds of the approaching crowd captured their attention.

Author and Bible teacher Rick Renner says of the soldiers sent to the garden:

The Greek word for "a band of men" is spira. This is the word that describes a military cohort—the group of 300 to 600 soldiers mentioned above. These extremely well-trained soldiers were equipped with the finest weaponry of the day.[60]

We also read that the soldiers were accompanied by "officers from the chief priests and Pharisees." Renner says:

> Once a judgment was given from the religious court of law, it was the responsibility of the temple police to execute these judgments. This fearsome armed force worked daily with the cohort stationed at the Tower of Antonia and reported to the chief priests, the Pharisees, and the Sanhedrin. These were the "officers" who accompanied the Roman soldiers to the Garden of Gethsemane. We can therefore conclude that when the Roman soldiers and temple police arrived to arrest Jesus, the hillside where the Garden was located was literally covered with Roman soldiers and highly trained militia from the Temple Mount.[61]

Apparently the hillside was crawling with soldiers who had been sent to arrest one man—One Man. The ebullient Judas walked up to Jesus and greeted Him with a kiss. When asked to identify himself, Jesus did so without hesitation, cautioning His disciples not to retaliate on His behalf. Jesus was then bound and marched back into Jerusalem, while Judas, the man who would be hero, followed along behind. Perhaps all dreams of glory evaporated as he trudged back across the foul Brook of Kidron awash in the blood of lambs and goats.

## JUDAS: THE BITTERNESS OF BETRAYAL

How soon after Jesus' arrest did Judas realize what a horrendous mistake he had made? Was it immediately following the capture? Was it as Jesus was being scourged? Was it when the soldiers ridiculed Him? We don't know the timing, but we do know that his remorse was crushing. Judas should not have been taken unawares at the consequences of his actions, but he was. Suddenly he realized that he had made the biggest blunder of his life: he had betrayed the Son of God into the hands of those who wanted only to kill Him. Beset with guilt he raced to the temple court, money bag in hand. "Stop!" he surely must have screamed. "This man is innocent!" But it was too late. Too late! The chief priests only laughed at him. They no longer had any use either for him or the tainted thirty pieces of silver. It was now blood money; it could not be returned to the temple coffers. Besides, what they wanted they now had: Jesus in their clutches.

Too late Judas realized that he had been a pawn in the hands of Satan; he had betrayed the One whose love was unconditional. He came face-to-face with the horrible deed he had done.

Persian poet and philosopher Omar Kayyám penned these poignant words:

> The Moving Finger writes; and, having writ,
>
> Moves on: nor all thy Piety nor Wit
>
> Shall lure it back to cancel half a Line,
>
> Nor all thy Tears wash out a Word of it."[62]

Possessed of the knowledge of his betrayal of the Son of God, Judas did the only thing he could think of to do at that moment; he threw the silver coins at the feet of the chief priests and raced out into the night. Matthew 27:5–8 (ESV) gives us a glimpse of the sad end to Judas' life:

> And throwing down the pieces of silver

into the temple, he departed, and he went and hanged himself. But the chief priests, taking the pieces of silver, said, "It is not lawful to put them into the treasury, since it is blood money." So they took counsel and bought with them the potter's field as a burial place for strangers. Therefore that field has been called the Field of Blood to this day.

Author and speaker Ray Pritchard wrote of Judas' desertion:

> In terms of experience, whatever you can say about James, Peter and John, you can say also about Judas. Everywhere they went, he also went. He was right there, always by the side of Jesus. He heard it all, saw it all, experienced it all. However you explain his defection, you cannot say he was less experienced than the other apostles.[63]

A line in the poem "Maud Muller" by John Greenleaf Whittier may well be applicable to Judas:

For of all sad words of tongue or pen,

The saddest are these: "It might have been!"[64]

# CHAPTER 16

*While he was still speaking, there came a crowd, and the*
*man called Judas, one of the twelve, was leading them.*
*He drew near to Jesus to kiss him, but Jesus said to him,*
*"Judas, would you betray the Son of Man with a kiss?"*

LUKE 22:47-48 ESV

The Roman soldiers and temple guard had arrested
the Man whom Judas kissed. As far as they were concerned, Jesus was the perpetrator, the rebel, the one whose
crimes had made Him a target of the chief priests. They
neither knew nor cared what He had done to raise the ire
of that august body, but they had done their job. Of course,
they had heard rumors of His antics—healings, the dead
raised to life, water turned to wine, and the way the people
praised Him as He rode into Jerusalem. Silly stories! Now
they were ready for a night of high jinks at the expense of
their captive. What they did not know as He was marched

off to the palace of Annas, the former high priest, was that this Man bound in the garden and led away as a criminal was the Lamb of God.

While awaiting a decision from High Priest Caiaphas and the Sanhedrin, the guards laid a fire in the courtyard to take away the chill of the night. It was there that Peter was challenged and denied knowing his Lord, not once, but three times, just as Jesus had prophesied. After having been found guilty of blasphemy, Jesus spent the night being mocked and goaded. At dawn, the taunting ceased; Jesus was dressed in His own clothing and taken to Pilate. The prelate swiftly determined that Jesus should be transferred to the jurisdiction of Herod Antipas, who, in turn, sent Him back to Pilate for sentencing.

## JESUS WAS SCOURGED

After being condemned to death, Jesus was scourged. That word alone fails to reveal the merciless beating that Jesus endured. William Barclay wrote, "Such scourging always preceded crucifixion and 'it reduced the naked body to strips of raw flesh, and inflamed and bleeding weals.' Men died under it, and men lost their reason under it, and few remained conscious to the end of it."[65]

The Roman scourge, also called the "fla-grum" or "flagellum" was a short whip made of two or three leather (ox-hide) thongs or ropes connected to a handle ... The leather thongs were knotted with a number of small pieces of metal, usually zinc and iron, attached at various intervals. Scourging would quickly remove the skin. According to history the punishment of a slave was particularly dreadful. The leather was knotted with bones, or heavy indented pieces of bronze.[66]

Jesus had been dragged before Pontius Pilate, convicted, and stripped of His outer garments. Roman soldiers had placed a wicked crown made of thorns on His head and proclaimed Him "King of the Jews." Mocking laughter reverberated through the palace halls as Jesus, the Galilean, was ridiculed. His raw and aching body bore the stripes that had been laid upon His back, and blood oozed from the cuts inflicted by the cat-o'-nine-tails applied during the lashing.

## THE ROAD TO GOLGOTHA

And then He was led away to Golgotha—the place of the skull, and there "the Darling of Heaven"[67] was crucified.

Jesus' words of forgiveness directed at those who crucified Him constitute the most powerful message ever spoken. It was nine o'clock in the morning on an otherwise ordinary day in Jerusalem. The sun was shining; the streets were filled with people going about their daily business. There was an underlying element of excitement. Word had spread that the Teacher had been arrested the night before and tried for blasphemy. Mobs had gathered to shout, "Crucify Him! Crucify Him!"

As shopkeepers opened their doors and raised their curtains, the sounds of marching feet and the noise of something heavy being dragged through the streets could be heard in the distance. Closer and closer they came, until the curious could at last see the soldiers who were driving a bloody and exhausted man toward the Damascus Gate. Across the road from the gate near the plot where the prophet Jeremiah was buried is a flat ledge atop the hill that resembles a skull. This was the Roman killing ground. Here criminals died, and the time had come. Three men were to be crucified that day. Two of them were thieves; the third was the Son of God.

The soldiers waiting on the hillside had likely been chosen at random. They were not Jews, as the men of Israel were exempted by Roman rules from serving in the military.

They may not even have been Romans, but rather conscripts rounded up from the four corners of the Roman Empire. It was just another day's work for them. They were on the crucifixion squad; it was not a pleasant task, but someone had to do it. The executioners were ready for the job at hand. Guilty—they didn't know or care. Innocent—maybe, maybe not. It was only a job.

Soon the mob exited the gate and crossed the road. Dragging the cross was a brawny man—a Cyrene, by the looks of him. A second man could be seen following him, trudging a few steps forward, then falling, only to be hauled upright and shoved another few steps along. He was totally unrecognizable. Isaiah the prophet had written, "He has no form or comeliness; and when we see Him, there is no beauty that we should desire Him" (Isaiah 53:2 NKJV).

That was certainly true of the man struggling to make His way to the place where the soldiers awaited. His back looked like shredded meat; His swollen face a series of bleeding holes where the crown of thorns had pierced His flesh; His beard had been torn out by its roots. He appeared to be more dead than alive. Accustomed to criminals fighting their destiny, the executioners rejoiced, as it meant the man now lying on the ground would be more easily subdued for the task at hand.

Roman philosopher Marcus Tullius Cicero wrote:

To bind a Roman citizen is a crime, to flog
him an abomination, to kill him is almost an
act of murder: to crucify him—What? There
is no fitting word that can possibly describe
so horrible a deed.[68]

## THE PLACE OF THE SKULL

On top of the hill, Simon, the Cyrene, dropped the cross to
the ground with a thud. Shuddering, he covered his face,
turned away, and stumbled to the sidelines. As he turned, he
was horrified to see that the body of Jesus had been dragged
upon the rough beam of the cross. His arms were stretched
to their limits, and ropes were being used to bind Him to the
crossbeam. Deftly, one of the executioners placed a spike
on Jesus' wrist, and then the hammer rang out, each stroke
securing the arm to the cross. The process was repeated on
the opposite arm, and then a spike was driven through His
feet that rested on a small platform.

With the spikes and ropes in place, the cross was raised
against the sky, and then, with a thud, it hurtled unimpeded
into the hole that would hold it upright. As the cross dropped
into the hole, the jarring collision of wood with earth ripped

flesh secured by the spikes. Some in the crowd looked upon Jesus—naked before the world, beaten to within an inch of His life, bruised and bloody—with satisfaction. Their purpose had been accomplished. I can easily imagine that Satan and all the demons in hell were dancing with glee. The Son of God was near death. The Enemy was certain he had won!

Mary, the mother of Jesus, and other bystanders bowed their heads in a mixture of love, shame, and compassion. Their beloved son, friend, offspring, and companion hung exposed to the world. Tears rolled down those faces, and sobs could be heard echoing from the hillside. As they watched in agony, the indifferent soldiers gathered in a circle at the foot of the cross. "Got any dice?" one might have called out. "Let's cast them for His clothes."

## FORGIVENESS BESTOWED

As they began to gamble, a whisper loud enough to ring through eternity issued from the mouth of Jesus, His first words spoken from the cross:

Father, forgive them, for they do not know what they are doing. Luke 23:34 NIV

Astonished, the soldiers halted their grisly game and

looked heavenward. They were accustomed to hearing screams and curses, pleas of innocence, entreaties for mercy, appeals for water, but a prayer for forgiveness—unimaginable! The Man on the cross had prayed for them, pleading for God's forgiveness for their actions.

The Son knew the Father in all of His mercy and His richly abounding love. He knew the words penned in Exodus:

> The Lord, the Lord, the compassionate and gracious God, slow to anger, abounding in love and faithfulness, maintaining love to thousands, and forgiving wickedness, rebellion and sin. Exodus 34:6–7 NIV

Did those men even know the name of the Man they had nailed to the cross—whose side they would pierce? Did they know His name was Jesus and that He was the Lamb of God, the One God had loved before the foundations of the world were even laid? It is likely none knew just how much they would need the forgiveness offered by the One hanging above them. They simply heard, "Father, forgive them, for they do not know what they are doing."

None understood that Jesus had taken on the role of advocate, defending the actions of those who had wronged Him. His teachings of "love your enemies, bless those who curse you, do good to those who hate you, and pray for those who spitefully use you and persecute you" (Matthew 5:44 NKJV) were more than mere utterances; they were a lifestyle. It was an act of the will. He was teaching the world about true forgiveness.

Jesus taught that there was a relationship between forgiving and receiving God's forgiveness:

> And whenever you stand praying, if you have anything against anyone, forgive him, that your Father in heaven may also forgive you your trespasses. But if you do not forgive, neither will your Father in heaven forgive your trespasses. Mark 11:25–26 NKJV

The prayer for forgiveness on the cross was not meant to be the last act of a dying man; it was an example for His followers. As they had been forgiven, so were they to forgive those who sinned against them. (See Matthew 6:9–13, the Lord's Prayer)

But God had a lesson, not only for Israel, for all mankind: He loved them with an everlasting love. It was a mirror of God's constant love that reaches far beyond our sinfulness all the way to the Cross, where Love hung between heaven and earth.

## THE THIRD HOUR

It was the third hour of the day. In the temple courtyard, the first of two daily sacrifices, the *Tamid*, or perpetual sacrifice, was prepared. In Exodus 29:38–39, 41–42 (NIV) we read:

> This is what you are to offer on the altar regularly each day: two lambs a year old. Offer one in the morning and the other at twilight. Sacrifice the other lamb at twilight with the same grain offering and its drink offering as in the morning—a pleasing aroma, a food offering presented to the Lord. For the generations to come this burnt offering is to be made regularly at the entrance to the tent of meeting, before the Lord.

These sin offerings were made as the first ceremony in the morning and the last at night. It was to be a constant reminder of sin and that the people could only be redeemed by a blood sacrifice. According to the Temple Institute, two lambs had been chosen:

> Although the lamb which had been selected for the tamid sacrifice had already been ascertained as being free of any

disqualifying blemish, nonetheless as an added precaution—since the Bible strongly prohibits the offering of blemished animals— it is checked again now by torchlight, after its removal from the chamber. This is to preclude the unlikely event that perhaps something has befallen it since it was last examined, which would render it unfit.

After it has been selected, the lamb is given to drink before it is slaughtered, for this makes its skin easier to remove. It is watered from a golden vessel; everything done in the Temple was always conducted with as much honor as possible.[69]

One of Jesus' utterances from the cross was, "I am thirsty" (John 19:28). Just as the sacrificial lamb was given water to drink, so was the Lamb of God offered liquid. Alfred Edersheim wrote of the daily sacrifices:

> The sacrifice was held together by its feet, the fore and hind feet of each side being tied together; its head was laid towards the south and fastened through a ring, and its face turned to the west, while the sacrificing

priest stood on the east side. The elders who carried the keys now gave the order for opening the Temple gates. As the last great gate slowly moved on its hinges, the priests, on a signal given, blew three blasts on their silver trumpets, summoning the Levites and the 'representatives' of the people (the so-called 'stationary men') to their duties, and announcing to the city that the morning sacrifice was about to be offered. Immediately upon this the great gates which led into the Holy Place itself were opened to admit the priests who were to cleanse the candlestick and the altar of incense.[70]

After whispering, "I thirst," John tells us, "When Jesus had received the sour wine, He said, 'It is finished,' and bowing His head, He gave up His spirit" (John 19:30 NKJV).

## THE EARTH HIDES ITS FACE

From noon until the sixth hour, or about three o'clock in the afternoon, "darkness came over all the land" (Matthew 27:45). Rev. Lonnie Branam, pastor of San Fernando Church of Christ, wrote of this phenomenon:

I would suggest that God darkened the earth in broad daylight because the last dying moments of Christ's life was too sacred for human eyes to see. Normally, we don't want a crowd around a loved one who is struggling for breath and about to die. This is a private moment in every person's life. The presence of loved ones and dearest friends is fitting, but around Christ that day was an irreverent crowd of revelers, skeptics, scoffers and unbelievers who couldn't wait for Him to draw His last breath. They had stripped Him nearly naked and gambled for the very clothes that were on His back. That darkness was a sacred concealment of the wounded body of Jesus, wounded even for all those around Him who hated Him and wanted Him dead. Thus it was most fitting that God should cover Him, hide Him away from brutal eyes that they might not see all that He suffered when He was made sin for us. Suffice it to say that the last three hours of the Lord's sufferings was far too sacred us know for human eyes to see. None of us who believe in Him will ever know just how sacred this scene was.[71]

It was about the sixth hour that the second daily sacrifice was brought into the temple courtyard and tied to the altar in readiness for the evening rite that was to occur at the ninth hour, the time that Jesus "gave up his spirit" (Matthew 27:50). It was also at that moment that "the curtain of the temple was torn in two from top to bottom. The earth shook, the rocks split and the tombs broke open" (Matthew 27:51–52 NIV).

The ninth hour has significance throughout both the Old and New Testaments, for it was then that Elijah stood on Mount Carmel before the prophets of Baal and petitioned God to send fire from heaven (see 1 Kings 18). Daniel was praying at the ninth hour when God sent Gabriel to answer his request (see Daniel 9:21). The first miracle by the apostles was wrought by Peter and John when they went to the temple to pray at the ninth hour (see Acts 3:1). And it was about the ninth hour that Cornelius prayed and an angel of the Lord told him to send for Peter (see Acts 10:3). It is a difficult note to include, for when Jesus prayed at the ninth hour, "My God, my God, why have you forsaken me?" the Father turned away from the sight of my sins and your sins hanging on the cross. He had to forsake His only begotten Son.

When Jesus breathed His last breath and willingly relinquished His spirit, Matthew tells us that "the veil of the temple was rent in twain from the top to the bottom" (Matthew 27:51 KJV). The high priest must have been terrified, but Jesus' work was finished.

Author and Bible scholar Charles Swindoll wrote:

> [Jesus] tilted His head back, pulled up one last time to draw breath and cried, "Tetelestai!" It was a Greek expression most everyone present would have understood. It was an accounting term. Archaeologists have found papyrus tax receipts with "Tetelestai" written across them, meaning "paid in full." With Jesus' last breath on the cross, He declared the debt of sin cancelled, completely satisfied. Nothing else required. Not good deeds. Not generous donations. Not penance or confession or baptism or ... or ... or ... nothing. The penalty for sin is death, and we were all born hopelessly in debt. He paid our debt in full by giving His life so that we might live forever.[72]

The Lamb of God had been offered sacrificially for the sins of all. As the high priest made his way into the Holy of Holies to sprinkle the blood of the evening sacrifice on the horns of the altar, the veil that separated man from God was ripped from top to bottom. It was a symbol that we no longer have to wait to be represented annually by the high priest:

> Seeing then that we have a great high priest, that is passed into the heavens, Jesus the Son of God, let us hold fast our profession. For we have not an high priest which cannot be touched with the feeling of our infirmities; but was in all points tempted like as we are, yet without sin. Let us therefore come boldly unto the throne of grace, that we may obtain mercy, and find grace to help in time of need.
>
> Hebrews 4:14–16 KJV

## ACCESS TO THE FATHER

Believers now have free access into the presence of God so that, "by prayer and supplication with thanksgiving let [our] requests be made known unto God" (Philippians 4:6 KJV).

The beautiful David Phelps song "End of the Beginning" says it all:

> And though He never ever did
>> a single thing wrong
> The angry crowd chose Him.

And then He walked down the

road and died on the cross

And that was the end of the beginning . . .

Three days later, He rose![73]

The work that Christ had been sent to do had been finished.

# CHAPTER 17

**REVELATION 19:4-16** NIV

The twenty-four elders and the four living creatures fell down and worshiped God, who was seated on the throne. And they cried:

"Amen, Hallelujah!"

Then a voice came from the throne, saying:

"Praise our God,
all you his servants,
you who fear him,
both great and small!"

Then I heard what sounded like a great multitude, like the roar of rushing waters and like loud peals of thunder, shouting:

"Hallelujah!

For our Lord God Almighty reigns.

Let us rejoice and be glad

and give him glory!

For the wedding of the Lamb has come,

and his bride has made herself ready.

Fine linen, bright and clean,

was given her to wear." (Fine linen stands

for the righteous acts of God's holy people.)

Then the angel said to me, "Write this: Blessed are those who are invited to the wedding supper of the Lamb!" And he added, "These are the true words of God."

At this I fell at his feet to worship him. But he said to me, "Don't do that! I am a fellow servant with you and with your brothers and sisters who hold to the testimony of Jesus. Worship God! For it is the Spirit of prophecy who bears testimony to Jesus."

## THE HEAVENLY WARRIOR DEFEATS THE BEAST

I saw heaven standing open and there before me was a white horse, whose rider is called Faithful and True. With justice he judges and wages war. His eyes are like blazing fire, and on his head are many crowns. He has a name written on him that no one knows but he himself. He is dressed in a robe dipped in blood, and his name is the Word of God. The armies of heaven were following him, riding on white horses and dressed in fine linen, white and clean. Coming out of his mouth is a sharp sword with which to strike down the nations. "He will rule them with an iron scepter." He treads the winepress of the fury of the wrath of God Almighty. On his robe and on his thigh he has this name written:

## KING OF KINGS AND LORD OF LORDS.

# ENDNOTES

1. James Strong, LL.D., S.T.D., *Strong's Exhaustive Bible Concordance* # H 4150, Hebrew and Aramaic Dictionary (Nashville, TN: Thomas Nelson Publishers, 1995), 74.

2. Ibid, #H 2287.

3. Dr. Jack Hayford, "The Beauty of Worship," http://www.jackhayford.com/pages/foundations_of_worship/beauty_of_worship.html; accessed February 2016.

4. Rev. George Warnock, "Hyssop—and the Passover," http://www.sermonindex.net/modules/articles/index.php?view=article&aid=953; accessed March 2016.

5. Tracey R. Rich, Judaism 101, "Pesach: Passover," http://www.jewfaq.org/holidaya.htm; accessed March 2016.

6. Ibid.

7. Rabbi Nosson Scherman, http://www.heritage.org.il/innernet/archives/4questions.htm; accessed March 2016.

8. "The Seder Service in a Nutshell," http://www.chabad.org/holidays/passover/pesach_cdo/aid/1751/jewish/The-Seder-in-a-Nutshell.htm; accessed March 2016.

9. Sam Nadler, *Messiah in the Feasts of Israel* (Charlotte, NC: Word of Messiah Ministries, 2006), 56.

10. Gilad Barach is a fourth-year student in Yeshiva College, majoring in physics and mathematics, and is a staff writer for *Kol Hamevaser*, "The Meaning of 'Next Year in Jerusalem,'" http://www.kolhamevaser.com/2014/04/the-meaning-of-next-year-in-jerusalem/; accessed March 2016.

11. Harold Hoehner, "Chronological Aspects of the Life of Christ," *Bibliotheca Sacra (A quarterly publication of Dallas Theological Seminary)* Volume 131, Issue 523, 1974.

12. Ken Ham, "Slain from the foundation of the world," April 7, 2007, https://answersingenesis.org/ministry-news/creation-museum/slain-from-the-foundation-of-the-world/; accessed April 2016.

13. Willmore D. Eva, "Editorial: Remembering from whence we came," *Ministry*, January 2000, https://www.ministrymagazine.org/archive/2000/01/remembering-from-whence-we-came.html; accessed March 2016.

14. Edward Chumney, *The Seven Festivals of the Messiah* (Shippensburg, PA: Treasure House, an imprint of Destiny Image Publishers, Inc., 1994), 59.

15. Ian Gordon, "The Burial—Jesus in the Feast of Unleavened Bread," http://www.jesusplusnothing.com/studies/online/FeastOfUnleavenedBread.htm; accessed June 2015.

16. John Metzger, "The Feast of First Fruits," http://promisestoisrael.org/jewish-culture-2/jewish-holidays/the-feast-of-first-fruits/; accessed March 2016.

17. C. W. Slemming, *Thus Shalt Thou Serve: The Feasts and Offerings of Ancient Israel* (Fort Washington, PA: CLC Publications, 1974), 123.

18. Mark Robinson, "Feast of Shavuot," http://www.jewishawareness.org/feast-of-shavuot/; accessed April 2016.

19. Dr. Randall Price, *Rose Guide to the Temple* (Torrance, CA: Rose Publishing, Inc., 2012), 46.

20. Rev. Mark Robinson, "Feast of Shavuot," February 7, 2014, http://www. jewishawareness.org/feast-of-shavuot/; accessed May 2015.

21. Iain Gordon, "The Feasts of the Lord: The Rapture—Jesus in the Feast of Trumpets," http://jesusplusnothing.com/studies/online/FeastOfTrumpets.htm; accessed April 2016.

22. *Rose Guide to the Tabernacle* (Torrance, CA: Rose Publishing, Inc., 2008), 110.

23. "Shofar," http://en.wikipedia.org/wiki/Shofar; accessed May 2015.

24. "Rosh Hashanah," http://www.aish.com/h/hh/rh/shofar/Shofar_Symbolism. html; accessed May 2015.

25. Nadler, 118.

26. Hugh Stowell, in *The Winter's Wreath, a Collection of Original Contributions in Prose and Verse,* 1828. Stowell rewrote & republished the words in 1831, http://www.cyberhymnal.org/htm/f/r/fromevsw.htm; accessed April 2015.

27. S. Michael Houdmann, "What is the difference between iniquity, sin, and transgression?" Got Questions Ministries, http://www.gotquestions.org/iniquity-sin-transgression.html; accessed March 2016.

28. David E. Lister, "Jesus our High Priest—The Day of Atonement," http://www. moriel.org/articles/sermons/jesus_our_high_priest.htm#; accessed June 2015.

29. Nadler, 137.

30. Charles Swindoll, "Jealousy," June 4, 2009, *Insight for Living Ministries,* https://sites.google.com/a/coalvilleumc.org/newcoalville/blog-and-announcements/jealousybycharlesrswindoll accessed February 2015.

31. John MacArthur, Jr., *The MacArthur New Testament Commentary,* (Chicago, IL: Moody Press 1983–2007).

32. Words by Fanny Crosby, http://wordwisehymns.com/2013/09/30/redeemed-how-i-love-to-proclaim-it/; accessed June 2015.

33. https://en.wikipedia.org/wiki/Lulav; accessed April 2016.

34. Slemming, 161.

35. Ibid, 162.

36. Alfred Edersheim, *The Life and Times of Jesus the Messiah,* eBook, *Book V, The Cross and the Crown,* Chapter 1, The First Day in Passion-Week, Palm-Sunday, http://philologos.org/__eb-lat/book501.htm; accessed July 2015,

37. Chuck Warnock, "Palm Sunday Sermon: On the Road to Calvary," March 27, 2010, https://chuckwarnockblog.wordpress.com/2010/03/27/palm-sunday-sermon-on-the-road-to-calvary/; accessed July 2015.

38. Teddy Kollek and Moshe Pearlman, *Jerusalem Sacred City of Mankind: A History of Forty Centuries* (New York, NY: Random House, 1972), 113.

39. John MacArthur, "The Righteous Anger of Jesus," http://www.gty.org/resources/bible-qna/BQ061312/the-righteous-anger-of-jesus; accessed April 2016.

40. Charles Swindoll, "The Gathering Storm," http://www.insight.org/resources/article-library/individual/the-gathering-storm; accessed July 2015.

41. Eric Lenhart, "Jesus Clears the Temple," http://www.sermoncentral.com/sermons/monday-8211-8220jesus-clears-the-temple8221-eric-lenhart-sermon-on-passion-of-christ-149286.asp?Page=1; accessed April 2016.

42. William Barclay, *The Gospel of Matthew, Volume 2* (Philadelphia, PA: The Westminster Press, 1958), 275.

43. William Barclay, *The Gospel of Matthew Volume 2* (Philadelphia, PA: The Westminster Press and Edinburgh, Scotland: The Saint Andrews Press, 1957), 281.

44. Barclay, 319.

45. Dr. John F. Walvoord, "23. Jesus Condemns the Scribes and Pharisees," https://bible.org/seriespage/23-jesus-condemns-scribes-and-pharisees; accessed July 2015.

46. http://www.forumancientcoins.com/catalog/roman-and-greek-coins.asp?vpar=812; accessed July 2015.

47. 2 Peter 3:9 KJV

48. Dante Gabriel Rossetti, "The House of Life," http://www.goodreads.com/quotes/tag/missed-opportunities; accessed April 2016.

49. Barclay, 337.

50. Ibid.

51. George Eldon Ladd, *A Theology of the New Testament* (Grand Rapids, MI: William B. Eerdmans Publishing Co., 1974), 196.

52. Author Unknown, "Judas' Motives and Role," http://www.ciu.edu/sites/default/files/Article/2010/11/JUDAS'%20MOTIVES%20AND%20ROLE/article349_terryhulbert_pdf_19778.pdf; accessed April 2016.

53. Max Lucado, *You'll Get Through This: Hope and Help for Your Turbulent Times* (Nashville, TN: Thomas Nelson Publishers, 2013), 7.

54. http://christiantimelines.com/marks_house.htm; accessed April 2016.

55. Rev. Randy Moll, "Lenten Devotions from Isaiah 53," http://www.goodshepherdrogers.org/tag/sacrifice/; accessed April 2015.

56. "Holy Week III: The Passover Meal," http://www.fishingtheabyss.com/archives/578; accessed April 2015.

57. Rev. John MacArthur, "Celebrating the Passover," http://www.gty.org/blog/B130327; accessed April 2015.

58. https://en.wikipedia.org/wiki/There_Is_a_Fountain_Filled_with_Blood; accessed July 2015.

59. Rev. John MacArthur, "A Place Called Gethsemane," http://sermonnotebook.org/mark/Mark%2072%20-%20Mark%2014_32-41.htm; accessed July 2015.

60. Rick Renner, "How Many Soldiers Does It Take To Arrest One Man?" http://www.cfaith.com/index.php/article-display/31-articles/easter/15779-how-many-soldiers-does-it-take-to-arrest-one-man; accessed July 2015.

61. Ibid.

62. http://www.goodreads.com/quotes/14196-the-moving-finger-writes-and-having-writ-moves-on-nor; accessed April 2016.

63. Ray Pritchard, "What Happened to Judas?" http://www.crosswalk.com/church/pastors-or-leadership/what-happened-to-judas-11532302.html?p=2; accessed July 2015.

64. John Greenleaf Whittier, "Maud Muller," http://www.poetry-archive.com/w/maud_muller.html; accessed July 2015.

65. Barclay, 400.

66. Bible History Online, "The Roman Scourge," http://www.bible-history.com/past/flagrum.html; accessed February 2013.

67. Darlene Zschech, "Worthy Is the Lamb," http://www.lyricsmode.com/lyrics/d/darlene_zschech/worthy_is_the_lamb.html; accessed February 2013.

68. Michael Licona, *The Resurrection of Jesus: A New Historiographical Approach* (Downers Grove, IL: InterVarsity Press, 2010), 304.

69. "A Day in the Holy Temple," http://www.templeinstitute.org/day_in_life/chamber_of_lambs.htm; accessed August 2015.

70. Alfred Edersheim, "The Temple—Its Ministry and Services," http://philologos.org/__eb-ttms/temple08.htm.

71. Lonnie Branam, "The Three Hours' Darkness," http://sanfernandochurchofchrist.com/SermonView.aspx?ID=840; accessed August 2015.

72. http://www.goodreads.com/quotes/tag/crucifixion; accessed April 2016.

73. Writer: David Phelps, Copyright: Winkin Music, Soulwriter Music Co. Inc., http://www.songlyrics.com/david-phelps/end-of-the-beginning-lyrics/#3zwiBvW6dRwwQoXq.99; accessed August 2015.

MICHAEL DAVID EVANS, the #1 *New York Times* bestselling author, is an award-winning journalist/Middle East analyst. Dr. Evans has appeared on hundreds of network television and radio shows including *Good Morning America, Crossfire* and *Nightline*, and *The Rush Limbaugh Show*, and on Fox Network, *CNN World News*, NBC, ABC, and CBS. His articles have been published in the *Wall Street Journal, USA Today, Washington Times, Jerusalem Post* and newspapers worldwide. More than twenty-five million copies of his books are in print, and he is the award-winning producer of nine documentaries based on his books.

Dr. Evans is considered one of the world's leading experts on Israel and the Middle East, and is one of the most sought-after speakers on that subject. He is the chairman of the board of the Ten Boom Holocaust Museum in Haarlem, Holland, and is the founder of Israel's first Christian museum—Friends of Zion: Heroes and History—in Jerusalem.

Dr. Evans has authored a number of books including: *History of Christian Zionism, Showdown with Nuclear Iran, Atomic Iran, The Next Move Beyond Iraq, The Final Move Beyond Iraq*, and *Countdown*. His body of work also includes the novels *Seven Days, GameChanger, The Samson Option, The Four Horsemen, The Locket, Born Again: 1967*, and *The Columbus Code*.

✦ ✦ ✦

Michael David Evans is available to speak or for interviews.
Contact: EVENTS@drmichaeldevans.com.

# BOOKS BY: MIKE EVANS

Israel: America's Key to Survival

Save Jerusalem

The Return

Jerusalem D.C.

Purity and Peace of Mind

Who Cries for the Hurting?

Living Fear Free

I Shall Not Want

Let My People Go

Jerusalem Betrayed

Seven Years of Shaking: A Vision

The Nuclear Bomb of Islam

Jerusalem Prophecies

Pray For Peace of Jerusalem

America's War:
The Beginning of the End

The Jerusalem Scroll

The Prayer of David

The Unanswered Prayers of Jesus

God Wrestling

The American Prophecies

Beyond Iraq: The Next Move

The Final Move beyond Iraq

Showdown with Nuclear Iran

Jimmy Carter: The Liberal Left
and World Chaos

Atomic Iran

Cursed

Betrayed

The Light

Corrie's Reflections & Meditations

The Revolution

The Final Generation

Seven Days

The Locket

Persia: The Final Jihad

**GAMECHANGER SERIES:**

GameChanger

Samson Option

The Four Horsemen

**THE PROTOCOLS SERIES:**

The Protocols

The Candidate

Jerusalem

The History of Christian Zionism

Countdown

Ten Boom: Betsie, Promise of God

Commanded Blessing

Born Again: 1948

Born Again: 1967

Presidents in Prophecy

Stand with Israel

Prayer, Power and Purpose

Turning Your Pain Into Gain

Christopher Columbus, Secret Jew

Living in the F.O.G.

Finding Favor with God

Finding Favor with Man

Unleashing God's Favor

The Jewish State: The Volunteers

See You in New York

Friends of Zion: Patterson & Wingate

The Columbus Code

The Temple

Satan, You Can't Have My Country!

Satan, You Can't Have Israel!

Lights in the Darkness

The Seven Feasts of Israel

**COMING SOON:**

Netanyahu

The Church

TO PURCHASE, CONTACT: orders@timeworthybooks.
com P. O. BOX 30000, PHOENIX, AZ 85046